In *Canyon of Hope,* Eric Donoho delivers a powerful, inspiring p̶
story that is engaging and profoundly insightful. With humble and
empathetic storytelling, Eric explores the lessons of resilience, showing
how faith, sustained by the powers of love, gratitude, and commitment,
drives us forward. His narrative, clear and compelling, guides readers
through an uplifting and thought-provoking journey. *Canyon of Hope* is not
just a book; it's a heartfelt reminder of the strength we find in our faith,
our bonds with others, and the transformative power of a hopeful spirit. A
must-read for anyone seeking inspiration.

— COLONEL VAL KEAVENY, US Army (Retired)

Eric is a great story-teller who does not shy away from his own brokenness
and darkness. Though his combat experiences in Iraq are a part of his story,
he shows us the other battles that are often harder to deal with: loss of
friends, poor health, and a marriage on the rocks. We get to see how faith,
friendship, and family build him up and sustain him on his journey from
darkness to dawn. **This book deeply resonated with me and gave me words
to both describe some of my own battles and help me with my own journey.**

— LIEUTENANT COLONEL BEN MEIER, U.S. Army

Canyon of Hope is an inspiring and heartfelt must-read. Relating to the
commonalities of another's struggles and challenges transitioning to civilian
life both personally and within family life. As Dustin's sister, these stories were
our real life; the good and the bad. This book will clearly connect with other
readers as the stories of success and pain transcend into everyone's life.

— AMY ROHDE

He returned from Iraq with unseen combat injuries which nearly ended his life
after coming home. He faced down his challenges with strength and resilience,
and he emerged a stronger husband and father as well as a committed advocate
for the most impactful veteran's legislation in a generation. This book is a must-
read for anyone seeking inspiration and to better understand the challenges
faced by many post-9/11 veterans when they transition home.

— CAPTAIN TOM PORTER, US Navy (Retired), National Veterans and Military Advocate

In this book, Eric doesn't sugar coat the raw emotions of the sacrifice not
only he went through to serve our country, but also his families. He dives
into suicide, miscarriage, and marital strife — things many times our
society doesn't allow us to grieve outwardly. If this book saves one other
man's life — and I believe it will - he has carried out his mission.

— LANAE STROVERS, President The Final Salute

Canyon of Hope is a profound and inspiring memoir that chronicles Eric Donoho's remarkable journey from the depths of despair to finding hope and resilience. As a veteran who faced immense personal and physical challenges, Eric's story is a testament to the power of vulnerability, faith, and the human spirit.

Eric's raw honesty in sharing his struggles with mental health, trauma, and chronic illness is both heartbreaking and uplifting. The book takes readers on an emotional rollercoaster, but ultimately leaves them with a profound sense of hope. His willingness to confront his darkest moments and find the strength to keep moving forward is truly admirable.

What sets this memoir apart is Eric's ability to weave his personal experiences with broader themes of community, advocacy, and the transformative power of giving back. His work with organizations like No Barriers and his advocacy efforts on Capitol Hill demonstrate how channeling one's pain into positive action can create meaningful change.

Eric's writing is engaging, vulnerable, and eloquent. He seamlessly blends his personal narrative with insights on faith, family, and the importance of holistic health. Readers will find themselves deeply invested in Eric's journey and inspired by his resilience. *Canyon of Hope* is a must-read for anyone seeking inspiration, guidance, or a reminder of the indomitable power of the human spirit.

Eric's story is a testament to the fact that no matter how dark the canyon, there is always a glimmer of hope on the horizon. This book is a gift to anyone who needs the courage to confront their own challenges and emerge stronger than ever before.

— HEATHER THOMSON, Entrepreneur, Co-Founder Beyond Fresh Organic Food Supplements, Consultant, Creative Director, Philanthropist, Real Housewives of New York

Eric brought both physical and mental wounds home from war but it's his journey of healing that makes his story an essential read.

— JAMES GEERING, Best Selling Author, Founder of *Behind the Shield* Podcast

Soldiers see war through a straw. Eric and I had different experiences from the same events. Through the grace of God and better wives than we deserve, we found success as civilians. *Canyon of Hope* is a story of success through faith. Anyone struggling to adjust after trauma will benefit from Eric's story and technique.

— SEAN MARSH, ESQ., Airborne, Ranger, Infantry turned Husband, Father, Lawyer

Eric has shared a very personal journey of how his courage, faith, hope and love has helped him overcome the challenges facing all too many veterans returning home. It takes a tremendous amount of courage to do what he did in defending freedom; however his insights help the reader to understand how much more courage is required to return home to normality after serving. He is incredibly open in explaining how he descended into such a desperate situation, but more importantly how he survived and continues to thrive because of his faith in God, hope in a better tomorrow, and the love of his family. His book helps bring to light the tragic reality of the mental health issues our returning service personnel continue to face.

— BRIAN WITTLER, ESQ., Owner Standard Barbers

Canyon of Hope is truly inspiring! Eric paints the picture, so you are along for this ride together. Vivid details allow you to feel his emotions and will pull yours out as well!

— BILL KRUEPER, Lieutenant Commander, US Navy (Retired)

Eric Donoho has learned that openness and vulnerability is a healing force that builds communities while restoring the health, authenticity and wholeness of the self. While we all work through the challenges and growing points of life, it's helpful to know that we're in it together. No one is immune to the pain points. Eric demonstrates how to face these pain points head-on, while learning how to navigate through them with truth, love and an awareness of our delicate humanity. Regardless of the struggle, we have the option to get up and see the potential and beauty in the next moment. These were my takeaways from *Canyon of Hope*.

— CONSTANCE BRENNEMAN, Actress, Producer, Director

This is a real story by an Army veteran who went to war on behalf of our country. It is a journey like so many others, where the call to duty is exciting and intense. But with repercussions of physical and mental trauma that lasts months and years longer, affecting our vets, their families and friends. This story is more than that...It is a deep and illuminating template for recovery that Eric has pieced together. He understands the pain and frustration of unresolved health issues that offer no easy solution. But all can learn from his experiences and concrete actions that are outlined in detail in this very important book.

— CURT VAN INWEGEN, CEO Life Elements

Eric's gripping journey through the highs and lows of life as a father, husband, soldier, and now veteran advocate is a powerful testament to the resilience of the human spirit. From our shared childhood in a small town Indiana to the harrowing moments in Iraq, where Eric endured multiple IED and rocket attacks, to the heartbreaking loss of his son, to cancer of his spouse, and to his own cancer diagnoses, and the loss of his dearest friend and confidant to suicide, Eric's memoir captures what drives all men to rise from their lowest points—the flicker of light and the love of family that guides them through the darkest of times.

As classmates from kindergarten to 12th grade, we shared grade school birthday parties to countless soccer games, and now as adults, and fathers, we share the profound bond of military service and raising our children in modern America.

Eric's unwavering fight to reclaim his life is profoundly inspirational and *Canyon of Hope* is blend of memoir and survival toolkit which offers a raw, honest account of love, redemption, and hope—a beacon for anyone facing life's toughest battles.

— BRENDAN MULLEN, Founder and CEO MKS2 Technologies,
Captain, US Army (Veteran)

Canyon of Hope is one of the most raw, humble and earnest reads you will ever read. Eric's journey is chronicled here, and it eloquently demonstrates that while we all have our own unique paths to walk, we, as humans, are not, and never have been truly alone. And it is in that commonality with mankind we find our greatest strength. Thank you, Eric, for your willingness and courage to remind us of all we are in this together.

— JAMES SALTER, 21 year Veteran Law Enforcement

Eric Donoho is not afraid to expose his heart in this masterful portrayal of his personal and powerful journey from darkness to dawn. *Canyon of Hope* proves that the human spirit is stronger than anything that can happen to it. Eric Donoho is a symbol that only the strongest souls are seared with the deepest scars.

— JASON VAN CAMP, Retired Special Forces Officer, Best Selling Author,
Executive Director Warrior Rising, Chairman Mission Six Zero

CANYON

of

HOPE

CANYON
of
HOPE

FROM DARKNESS TO DAWN
*Embracing the **Light Within***

ERIC B. DONOHO

Niche Pressworks
Indianapolis, IN

CANYON OF HOPE

For permission to reprint portions of this content or bulk purchases, contact info@handupllc.com

Published by Niche Pressworks; NichePressworks.com
Indianapolis, IN

ISBN
Hardcover: 978-1-962956-26-0
Paperback: 978-1-962956-25-3
eBook: 978-1-962956-27-7

Library of Congress Control Number: 2024915302

To Jenn, my beloved wife,
and my two amazing children, Kayleigh and Byron.

Jenn, from the depths of my heart, thank you for being my best friend, the love of my life, and my constant inspiration. Your unwavering support and boundless love have been my rock, guiding me through the stormiest seas. Because of you, I strive to reach new heights and become the best version of myself. Your love, compassion, and faith are the foundation of our family, and I am forever grateful for your presence in my life.

To Kayleigh and Byron, my dear children, thank you for being my literal lifesavers. Your smiles, laughter, and boundless curiosity have been the light in my darkest moments. You inspire me to be a better human being and face each day with courage and optimism. You are my world, my reason for everything, and my greatest source of joy and motivation.

This book is dedicated to you, my family, for your endless love, strength, and inspiration. It is a testament to the power of faith, love, and resilience. May it serve as a lighthouse of hope for others, showing that even in the darkest times, the light within us can guide us to a brighter dawn.

CONTENTS

Foreword

A NO BARRIERS LIFE

IN 2001, I became the first blind person in history to climb Mt. Everest. After descending safely back to basecamp, I was greeted with a hug and the prophetic words from our team leader, Pasquale "PV" Scatturo: "Don't make Everest the greatest thing you ever do."

It was poorly timed advice, but those words made a lasting impression on me and my teammates, those brothers who had surrounded me to reach the top of the world.

PV's words were not meant to squash our celebration; he simply wanted to convey that meaning doesn't necessarily come from what you've done, but from what you do with the experience.

No Barriers became the outpouring of that charge. Ten years after our historic Everest ascent, my team came together to give back to those who have served our country and returned — alive, but not whole. We recruited a team of eleven severely injured service men and women and climbed a twenty-thousand-foot peak in the Himalayas. One of the participants said that the expedition had done more for his personal growth than five years of therapy, and we knew that the power of the mountains, the camaraderie, and the bonds of shared hardship and love could transform in profound and unexpected ways. There was no magic pill, but summits would become the shining symbol to help others who have been shattered by war to heal, to reach, and to reclaim their lives and potential. Since that initial experience, No Barriers has led hundreds of veteran programs, and we improve a little each day.

I met Eric Donoho in 2016 during a desert trek through the Gila Wilderness for that year's Warriors program. Many veterans join our programs with severe physical injuries such as paralysis, missing limbs, and blindness. Others, like Eric, endure invisible disabilities. All carry the deep emotional and psychological wounds of conflict.

I don't believe that every challenge can be overcome, and No Barriers is not a battle cry for "anything is possible." Instead, what we teach and model is a mindset of growth and action and an intention to live with purpose. Just as PV suggested, meaning lies in how we descend from the mountain, take the lessons earned from our struggles, and use them to elevate our lives and communities.

In the years following our first meeting, Eric has represented No Barriers as a movement for our corporate sponsors and the public. His journey is a demonstration that we are united through challenge, both visible and invisible, and we are healed through action.

After the tragic loss of his dearest friend to suicide, Eric turned his sorrow to advocacy on Capitol Hill, where he championed crucial veteran-focused legislation such as the National Suicide Hotline Designation Act and the PACT Act — both issues that touched him personally.

Eric's journey, earnestly captured in *Canyon of Hope: From Darkness to Dawn; Embracing the Light Within,* is an example for each of us in embracing a No Barriers Life. As you dive into these pages, may the spirit of Eric's transformative journey inspire you to contemplate your own barriers and envision how you might leverage your challenges as stepping stones to a more fulfilling life. Obstacles will always exist, but as we say at No Barriers, "What's within you is stronger than what's in your way."

— **ERIK WEIHENMAYER**
American athlete, adventurer, and best-selling author
Co-founder of No Barriers

STANDING AT THE EDGE: A JOURNEY FROM DARKNESS TO DAWN

HAVE YOU EVER stood at the edge of a vast canyon and felt both awe and trepidation? The sheer drop, the expanse of rugged terrain, and the promise of a breathtaking sunrise on the horizon. This balance between darkness and dawn mirrors the journey many of us face in life, where hope must rise from the depths of despair.

The journey to writing *Canyon of Hope: From Darkness to Dawn; Embracing the Light Within* began in a place of profound darkness. Like many who have served in the military, I found myself facing challenges that seemed insurmountable. The weight of my experiences overseas, combined with personal struggles at home, often left me feeling isolated and overwhelmed. Yet, in those moments of despair, I discovered a flicker of hope that guided me toward healing and growth.

This book is the culmination of that journey. It's not just a recounting of my own path but a collection of insights, stories, and tools designed to help others find the flicker of light in their own life. It's a guide for those standing at the crossroads, uncertain of which path to take. Drawing from my own experiences, this book aims to illuminate the strength and resilience found in choosing to thrive amid adversity.

If you are a service member who has faced significant challenges and are now navigating the path to recovery, or if you are currently struggling with the weight of those experiences, please know there is hope and a way forward. If you are the spouse or partner of a service member, I hope these stories provide you with understanding and support, reminding you that you are not alone. The journey of healing and growth is a shared one, and together we can find strength in our experiences.

Within these pages, you will find that no matter how deep or dark your struggles, there is always a path back toward the light. This book showcases how embracing faith, gratitude, and the innate goodness of the human spirit can steer your life back on course. *Canyon of Hope* isn't just my story — it's a toolkit for overcoming adversity, discovering inner strength, embracing transformation, and reclaiming control over your destiny.

As you turn these pages, my hope is that you will discover the inspiration needed to navigate your own canyons. Together, we will explore the depths of our struggles and ascend to the peaks of our triumphs, embracing the light within us all.

Join me on this journey from darkness to dawn. Let's find hope and strength together, one step at a time.

Chapter *1*

THE WEIGHT OF BROKENNESS

LAUGHING AND BRIMMING with joy, my wife, our spirited four-year-old daughter, our one-year-old son in his big-boy stroller, and I were leaving our bungalow at the Fairmont Miramar Hotel & Bungalows in Santa Monica. The Fairmont had been a sanctuary during my wife's challenging breast cancer treatments at Cedar Sinai, but this visit was lighter, happier.

Exiting the grand lobby, we strolled into the circular driveway, admiring the majestic banyan tree before walking along the landscaped path adorned with towering palm trees and vibrant flowers. The kids were delighted, pointing at the bursts of pink and purple blooms.

As we walked through the huge wrought-iron gates at the end of the drive, we turned right onto Wilshire Boulevard, heading toward Ocean Avenue. The Pacific Ocean, visible in the distance, made the kids even more excited. Our daughter, Kayleigh, eyes wide with anticipation, said, "Daddy, look. There's the ocean! There's the beach!"

Holding her hand tightly, I smiled, feeling the warmth of the sun and her excitement. "I know, sweetie," I said. "We're almost there." Her joy was contagious, and we moved closer to the beach, ready to enjoy a beautiful day by the sea.

Suddenly, a wild convoy of motorcycles and jeeps, all modified with animal furs and goat-like devil horns, burst onto the street. The riders and drivers were clad in similar animal furs and leather outfits, bore tattoos of satanic symbols, and yelled and swore as they wove across the pavement.

I instinctively grabbed my daughter and reached for my wife and son, trying to shield them from the pandemonium. But before I could secure my grip, some of the motorcyclists broke through, snatched my wife and kids away, and threw them into a topless Jeep that sped south down Ocean Boulevard.

Panic surged through me, but I knew immediate action was crucial. Propelled by adrenaline, I sprinted after them. The trail of frightened pedestrians and disrupted traffic left in the gang's wake guided me as I desperately tried to keep up, determined to rescue my family from the clutches of these frightening strangers.

As I rounded a left turn and headed east, an unfamiliar and ominous neighborhood that looked like a warehouse district unfolded before me. In the distance, I spotted a heavily fortified compound where satanic music blared ominously. Participants in the frenzied escapade filled the streets, but amid the turmoil, I caught glimpses of my wife and kids.

Desperation set in as I frantically searched for something, anything, to use as a weapon. The bystanders nearby were of little help, standing motionless out of fear of becoming the next victims.

As I moved down the street, I spotted a man eyeing something in the corner of a nearby shop. It was a sword. My rational mind questioned the practicality of approaching armed kidnappers with a sword, but time was of the essence, and options were scarce. Without a second thought, I grabbed the sword, slung it across my back, and advanced toward the compound with a single focus: retrieve my family from this nightmarish ordeal.

As I positioned myself outside the compound, my military instincts took over. Recognizing that stealth was paramount, I decided my best strategy was to remain undetected, infiltrate under the cover of darkness, and extract my family with as little confrontation as possible.

As dusk turned to night and shadows lengthened into darkness, I used the opportunity to slip beneath a loosely secured section of the barbed-wire fence. The ground beneath was rough and unforgiving, but determination fueled my movements. Moving across the lawn, I stayed low, using the darkness as my ally, mindful that silence was crucial. The cool night air was punctuated by the distant sounds of chaotic revelry from within the compound.

I only encountered one guard who seemed to notice something amiss. With no choice but to engage, I quickly subdued him, ensuring he remained silent. I donned his outfit, disguising my identity to navigate the compound more freely. As I entered the building, I had no illusions about the danger ahead; it was going to be a relentless struggle for survival.

Each room I entered brought a new challenge, each corridor a potential ambush. Every confrontation was met with the necessary force to neutralize the threat, and I was always moving, always pushing forward. It was a harrowing journey through the heart of darkness. With each room cleared and each opponent dispatched, my resolve strengthened as I continued to be fueled by the urgent need to reunite with my loved ones and bring them to safety.

Reaching the top floor, I burst through the door into a harrowing scene. My children were locked in a cell, crying, as they watched their mother, who was bound and naked on an ominous altar. Her eyes met theirs, radiating calm despite the terror. "It'll be okay, kids," she reassured them softly, even as her own fear was palpable. "Just close your eyes; remember what we do when we're scared. We pray." As their small voices began to murmur prayers, I steeled myself and faced the leader of this hellish assembly, who was adorned with devil horns.

"You're tougher than I thought," he taunted, his voice echoing off the stark walls. "But today, you die."

I exhaled slowly, gripping my weapon. "Perhaps," I said, "but not before you. Let's finish this."

The battle was relentless. He was always one step ahead of me, predicting my every strike. Exhaustion crept in, clouding my judgment, pulling me deeper into despair — exactly where he wanted me. In a critical misstep, his blade found its mark, piercing my side. The pain was beyond any physical agony I'd experienced before. As I fell, the devil's laughter filled the room, chilling me to the bone.

"I said you would die today," he sneered, turning his attention back to my family.

With the cold floor against my back, I watched helplessly as my wife and children screamed, their faces stricken with horror. The sense of failure was overwhelming, a crushing weight that squeezed the life from me even faster than the blood escaping my wound. As darkness rimmed my vision, the last thing I saw was the tear-streaked faces of my family, their cries echoing in my fading consciousness.

My eyes snapped open to complete darkness. Sweat streamed down my face, my clothes and the bed beneath me soaked through — a testament to the intensity of the dream that haunted me once again. This recurring dream, the one where I never survive, had become a regular source of fear, filling my days with a constant sense of unease. Ever since I'd accidentally discovered my wife, Jenn, was contemplating divorce a few weeks before, my nightmares had become routine. I chose not to mention my discovery because, somehow, knowing her considerations without her awareness gave me a sense of control, an upper hand in navigating our future.

As I lay there, freshly shaken from my dream, I turned to watch Jenn sleeping peacefully beside me. Her calmness contrasted sharply with my inner turmoil, deepening my sense of inadequacy. Despite my best efforts, I'd failed to love her in the ways she needed. I hadn't been the supportive partner she deserved. I lacked in listening, understanding, and patience. Even in my role as a father, where I believed I was putting forth a good effort, I felt I was failing.

My continual nightmares and overwhelming sense of failure brought me to a harrowing conclusion: my family would be better off without me.

It wasn't about selfishness; I believed my absence would allow them to find happiness and flourish without me holding them back. Ending my life would free them from the fear and limitations my presence brought into their lives. It was how I could truly protect and show my love for my family. The peace this decision brought me allowed me to drift back to sleep, and before I knew it, Jenn's alarm was signaling the start of a new day. She rushed to get ready while I moved through my morning routine with a foreign sense of calm.

After a quick goodbye, Jenn was out the door, the garage door's rumble marking her departure. Just then, Kayleigh and my one-year-old son, Byron, woke up. As I lifted my son from his crib and reminded my daughter to head to the potty, I decided this morning was going to be special.

I changed my son and picked out his outfit along with extra clothes for daycare. As I moved to my daughter's room, I saw she was already lost in her imaginary world, dancing and giggling in front of the mirror. Not wanting to interrupt her joy, I quietly laid out her clothes and packed a spare outfit in her backpack. Downstairs, I prepared French toast for my daughter and ensured all snacks and bottles were ready for the day.

Sprinkling extra powdered sugar over her French toast, I turned to the task I usually dreaded: taming her long hair. It flowed past her waist and was often a source of morning battles. However, because we'd braided it tightly the night before, there were no knots. With no tangles to fight over, I styled her hair into two braids that joined into a single long braid at the back, making her feel like a princess for the day.

With hair done and breakfast finished, we headed out the door. Our Yukon Denali, affectionately known as the Silver Bullet, hummed warmly, ready for the chilly morning. After securing Byron in his car seat, I watched Kayleigh climb into her big girl seat, full of excitement for the Christmas gifts she was making for me and Jenn saying, "Daddy, I can't tell you what it is." I just smiled at her as I finished buckling her in and shut the door.

I hopped into the driver's seat and plugged in my iPhone, setting our favorite playlist to shuffle and filling the car with tunes that always made our drive to school a joyful ritual.

As our favorite songs played — Rodney Atkins's *Watching You* and Van Morrison's *Brown Eyed Girl* — the mood was light, but it was Alicia Keys's *Girl on Fire* that truly animated my daughter. Her voice soared, perfectly in tune, a stark contrast to my own, less-musical attempts. I found myself stopping mid-verse just to listen to her; the beauty of her voice made the drive feel all too brief. Soon, we were pulling into the daycare's parking lot.

Once we arrived at the church daycare, I juggled the bags on my shoulders, Byron in his car seat, and held Kayleigh's hand as we navigated the cold parking lot. Entering the building and walking past murals of animals, our conversation turned to the wonders of creation.

"Hey, Dad, did you know God made monkeys and zebras and giraffes? God made us too. He made everything. God is pretty cool, huh?" Kayleigh's innocent affirmation of faith made me smile despite the turmoil inside me. It was a relief to know my struggles with faith hadn't touched her.

Byron's drop-off was smooth sailing. I helped him out of his car seat and hugged him tightly before he eagerly toddled off to join his classmates. Now, it was time for the part of our morning ritual I cherished most: the playful race between Kayleigh and me from Byron's class to hers. This part of our day involved a sprint up a notably steep flight of stairs. Kayleigh loved the element of surprise, often shouting "Go!" when I least expected it, securing herself a generous head start. Today was no different.

As she darted away with a shout, we raced through the hallway, then charged up the stairs. Her classroom was directly above Byron's, making our route a loop back to where we'd started. She reached the finish line ahead of me, her face lit up with a victorious grin. "Daddy, I beat you!" she exclaimed joyfully.

"I know, sweetie! Good job! I'm so proud of you," I said, my voice cheerful yet thick with emotion. As we organized her belongings on her hook and stowed them in her cubby, I bent down to give her a particularly tight hug. Knowing this was my final morning with her made it hard to let go.

"Dad, that was a really tight hug. I loved it!" she said, her words pulling a bittersweet smile across my face.

Reluctantly releasing her, I watched as she skipped into her classroom. I lingered for a moment, then walked back down the hall, descending the stairs to the parking lot. My steps were heavy as I approached the Silver Bullet.

As I drove, my usual mental checklist was conspicuously absent. There were no tasks vying for attention, no family errands ticking away in the back of my mind — just an unsettling stillness. My decision cast a shadow over everything. Convinced that today would be my last, I didn't even bother to plug in my iPhone, and the quiet was pervasive, enveloping.

When I pulled up to our house, I parked the car on the driveway and made a beeline for the front door. My hand shook slightly as I inserted my key into the lock. Then, I pushed the door open and stepped into the entryway of our home. I quickly climbed the stairs to our master bedroom and went straight to the nightstand by our bed, pulled open the top drawer, and pressed my right index finger against the biometric safe hidden inside. It clicked open, and I retrieved my Glock and its magazine. After closing the safe and the drawer, I walked back to the hallway, descended the stairs with heavy steps, and entered the kitchen.

Sitting at the kitchen table I'd built months earlier, I methodically loaded the magazine into the Glock, chambered a round, and placed the muzzle against my lips. I slowly opened my mouth and felt the cold metal scraping against my teeth, the faint taste of gunpowder lingering from my last visit to the range. I closed my eyes, the weight of my decision pressing down on me.

As I slid my finger from the trigger guard to the trigger itself, I felt a sensation I hadn't experienced before, an eerie presence, as if something were there with me. My finger met the trigger, and I began to squeeze, but it refused to move. I tried again and again, each attempt failing to engage the trigger mechanism, adding to my frustration. *How can I fail at something as simple as this?* I thought bitterly.

Dismayed, I removed the Glock from my mouth and began to disassemble it. The trigger mechanism didn't appear to have any obstructions or faults. Reassembling the weapon, I dry-fired it successfully. Reinserting the magazine and chambering a round, I returned the gun to my mouth, but still, the trigger wouldn't budge. It felt like an invisible force was intervening, preventing me from pulling it.

Hours passed in this surreal state until a glance at the stove clock reminded me it was time to pick up my children from daycare. The realization that I had responsibilities waiting, that I couldn't let them down again, pierced through my despair. *Maybe this failure is a sign,* I thought. *Maybe I should spare my family the horror of finding me here in our home, a place that would be tainted by such a tragedy.*

Resigned, I cleared the Glock once more, removed the magazine, and returned both to the safe. After taking a few moments to gather myself, I drove to the daycare.

Picking up my kids shifted my focus. My daughter's chatter about her day and her excitement over upcoming Christmas surprises brought a semblance of normalcy. Despite the darkness that had enveloped me, their presence, their innocence, and their needs reminded me of my role as their father. My job was not just to provide but to be present and ensure their happiness. As we drove home, the weight of my actions hung over me. But hearing my son laugh and seeing my daughter's bright eyes in the rearview mirror, I felt a sliver of relief. Maybe, just maybe, failing to pull that trigger was the moment I needed to rethink everything — not just for my sake, but for theirs.

Two days after my failed suicide attempt, I received devastating news: my first platoon sergeant, the man who'd personally recruited me into the scout sniper platoon, attended my wedding, and supported me during our early family traumas, had taken his own life. We'd drifted apart after a disagreement, yet his death struck me profoundly.

He was the thirteenth person I'd known who had succumbed to such a fate, but his loss hit closest to home.

As I dwelled on the situation, my anger shifted inward. Why hadn't I reached out? Could a simple phone call have changed the trajectory of either of our lives? The realization of our shared struggles and the missed opportunity for mutual support was a bitter pill to swallow. His actions mirrored the path I was on, poised to inflict the same pain and sorrow on my family that his passing brought to his loved ones and me.

This parallel forced me to confront my own vulnerabilities and the fragility of life itself. The turmoil of sleepless nights and a mind racing with *what-ifs* highlighted the precariousness of my mental state. His death served as a grim reminder of the destructive potential of the path I was contemplating, pushing me to question the legacy I intended to leave behind.

Well after midnight, with the world asleep and my struggles at their peak, I found myself watching *Rocky* on TBS. Rocky's words struck a chord deep within me: "You, me, or nobody is gonna hit as hard as life. But it ain't about how hard you hit. It's about how hard you can get hit and keep moving forward; how much you can take and keep moving forward. That's how winning is done!" I realized I'd stopped fighting back against life's blows. I'd allowed the darkness to pin me down, to dictate my worth and my actions.

Seeking a new path and a way to rectify my past mistakes, I knew I needed change and a better way forward — one that would keep me here to fix the chaos I had created. I knew if I confided in Jenn, her immediate response would be to have me check into a VA hospital, but deep down, I felt that wasn't the right step for me. Instead, I reached out to my best friend, Brent, knowing he would be awake due to the time difference between Indiana and Alaska.

Brent answered the phone with his usual humorous greeting, "Bill's Backyard Barbecue and Grill, what can I get you?" After letting the silence hang between us for a few moments, he asked if everything was okay.

"Brent, I tried to eat my Glock two days ago. I don't want to die; I need help," I said.

There was a heavy silence that felt like it stretched on forever before he finally responded, "It's all good, brother. I got you. What's going on? What do you need?"

As I unloaded years of bottled-up turmoil, each revelation wasn't met with judgment or panic but with a calm, "Okay, we can deal with that." His reassurances gave me space to breathe and hope for a future beyond the pain. Our conversation meandered into the early hours, plotting a course through the fog that had settled over my life. Brent's unwavering support, his insistence on a tangible plan, was a lifeline thrown into the tumultuous sea of my thoughts. His challenge, for me to apply to No Barriers Warriors, was not just about climbing mountains; it was an invitation to reclaim my life, to prove to myself that I could rise above the despair that threatened to consume me.

As our call ended, gratitude for Brent's presence and his refusal to let me face my demons alone filled my bucket, which had been empty for an incredibly long time. His affirmation, "You're like my little brother; I got you," was more than just words; it was a pledge of solidarity, a reminder that no matter how isolating the darkness feels, we are never truly alone in our battles.

My heart-to-heart with Brent shifted something funda-mental within me. It was as if confessing the storm within had dissipated some of its fury. Perhaps it was the sheer re-lief of not having to mask my turmoil from him, or maybe it was the tangible steps toward change we had plotted out, but either way, the burden I'd been carrying felt lighter, making room for a sliver of hope that perhaps, change was within reach.

This book illustrates that no matter how deep and dark the hole you've dug, there is always light and a path up-ward. It's not merely a recount of my journey, but a road-map showing how you can harness the power within yourself to overcome the anger and fear driving your life off course. By embracing faith and gratitude and acknowl-edging the goodness of the human spirit, you can trans-form everything.

Chapter 2

LOVE AT FIRST FLIGHT

WHEN I ENLISTED in the military in 2004, I aspired to be an Airborne Infantryman with the hopes of one day earning my Ranger Tab and the coveted Green Beret. Once I finished Airborne School, I had the chance to spend some quality time back home with family and friends in Indiana before I was due to report to my first duty station at Fort Richardson. It was during this period that I managed to catch up on movies I'd missed while busy with basic training, infantry training, and Airborne School.

One movie, *A Lot Like Love*, featuring Ashton Kutcher and Amanda Peet, really caught my attention. The plot kicks off with their characters striking up an impromptu connection at the airport, which swiftly escalates to a spontaneous rendezvous in the airplane lavatory. This scene hooked me, and despite the movie being a run-of-the-mill rom-com, I couldn't stop watching as I finished packing for my departure to Anchorage.

My parents and I set out for South Bend Regional Airport early in the morning on June 8, 2004. After a brief meal together at the airport café, we shared heartfelt good-byes before I passed through the TSA checkpoint and gave them one final wave. The first leg of my journey took me from South Bend to Indianapolis, then on to Atlanta, where I had some layover time to roam, grab a bite, and visit the United Service Organizations (USO) before my last flight to Anchorage. Boarding time arrived for my Delta flight, and I headed to my assigned seat, 14D, the middle seat in the middle row. Settling in, I found myself idly speculating about who might end up sitting beside me.

A LOT LIKE LOVE

Then, she boarded. A vision of beauty with long, dark, wavy hair, dressed in a chic, dark pinstripe suit, carrying a brown Bath and Body Works bag. Her smile, bright and inviting, illuminated the cabin. As she walked down the aisle, I began to hope she'd sit next to me. Despite real-izing I might be staring a bit too intently, I struggled to pull my eyes away, only to realize she was indeed taking the seat next to mine. I immediately thought of the movie I'd watched the day before, and I began panicking, out-wardly attempting to remain composed. As she sat down, I managed to muster up the courage to introduce myself and said, "Hi, my name is Eric. What's yours?"

She turned toward me, her sparkling hazel eyes meet-ing mine, and with a warm smile, she replied, "Hi Eric! My name is Jennifer, but you can call me Jenn."

Almost no time passed before Jenn and I were deeply engaged in conversation, laughing and sharing stories as if we were old friends rather than strangers. Her presence was captivating, and the buzz of the aircraft faded into the background as we talked. Despite the flight's attempt at a meal service, where the chicken in my chicken dinner was notably absent, and *Hitch* played on the big screen just in front of us, my attention kept drifting back to Jenn. Watching her reactions to the movie — her smiles and laughter — felt more entertaining than anything else. The accidental brushes of our arms or legs sent electrifying jolts through my body, a sensation both startling and ex-hilarating. I looked at my watch, desperately hoping time would slow down because I didn't want this flight to end. I fought to keep my eyes open to be able to enjoy every min-ute, but I eventually fell asleep leaning into the woman of my dreams.

Awakening as the cabin bustled in preparation for our descent into Anchorage, indecision plagued me over whether to share my number with Jenn. Seizing a moment of solitude when Jenn got up from her seat, I wrote my number on a small piece of paper, pocketing it just in case. In the final hour of our flight, Jenn's narratives unveiled her deep love for Anchorage. Her vivid descriptions, borne of a lifetime's acquaintance, lent a comforting familiarity to the unknown. As we neared our destination, we strained to look out the window, and I listened to Jenn's guided tour that highlighted landmarks and personal sanctuaries.

"There's Girdwood, home to Alyeska, Alaska's premier ski resort. The town of Indian is known for Indian Valley Meats and their exquisite smoked delicacies. That road tracing the ocean's edge? That's the Seward Highway, my sanctuary for contemplation, unrivaled in beauty. Potter

Marsh, where I wander with Brandy, my dog, in tow. And there's south Anchorage, leading us to our airport. We'll arc over the ocean, circling Fire Island for our approach," she shared. Her enthusiasm was infectious, casting a warm glow on my anticipations.

The landing was as smooth as the narrative Jenn had woven, drawing us gently back to earth. An ache of melancholy struck as we taxied to the north terminal. I knew the bond I'd formed with Jenn over the course of our flight was something special, and I wasn't ready to say goodbye. I lingered by her side as we strolled through the terminal, pausing at exhibits of Alaskan wildlife, each piece evoking a memory Jenn shared with animated grace. The descent down the two-story escalator to baggage claim was bittersweet. The weight of my decision — to share my contact or not — grew heavier with each step. Only as Jenn claimed her luggage did the realization that she was about to exit my life forever spur me into action.

I mustered my courage and said, "Jenn, before you go, if you would ever like to get together and do something, here is my cell number."

Jenn's eyes lit up. "Yes, I would absolutely love to see you again. Here is mine," she said, handing me a piece of paper.

"Do you want a ride to base?" she asked.

"Thank you so much for the offer, but I can't. I have someone coming to pick me up. So great meeting you!" I said.

"Have a great night," she said as I leaned in and gave her a friendly hug goodbye.

As I watched Jenn's figure disappear through the automatic doors, I realized her presence had shielded me from my underlying anxieties about stepping into a world that was entirely new and uncharted. My surroundings, now quiet as the bustling terminal began to empty, heightened my apprehension. Collecting a baggage cart and gathering my duffels, I inquired at a help desk about the USO's location and was directed outside toward the south terminal. When I exited the terminal, I was greeted by a sunlit sky, despite it being nearly midnight, and the Chugach Mountains painting a majestic backdrop against the lingering twilight. The walk to the south terminal became a moment of awe as I soaked in the novelty of my environment, the late hour illuminated by a sun that refused to set.

Upon reaching the USO, I learned that all the other servicemembers had already arrived, and everyone, including my Non-Commissioned Officer in Charge (NCOIC), had been waiting for me for some time — no one was thrilled. Once I arrived, we quickly walked through an underground passage leading us toward the awaiting transport. The route was lined with stuffed displays of Alaskan wildlife, their grandeur capturing my full attention, causing me to trail behind. The tunnel, gradually shedding its decorative guise, funneled us toward sliding doors, revealing a white government van waiting to ferry us to our new barracks. My heart beat with a blend of excitement and apprehension at the unknown stretching before me like the untraveled roads of Alaska.

I secured a window seat as we loaded into the van, a small victory that allowed me to take in the setting as we navigated the streets toward Fort Richardson. Our route took us through downtown Anchorage, the vibrant heart of the city. Lost in thought, the transition to Glenn Highway snapped me back to reality, signaling our approach to the base. The procedural formalities of base entry, accommodations, and the demeanor of my new Non-Commissioned Officers (NCO) whirled in my mind. As we veered onto the base access ramp, an NCO's command to ready our IDs confronted me with the immediate reality of military discipline and structure that awaited.

Time flew by during my first few days at Fort Richardson. I was swamped with duties, but in a rare moment of leisure after a run to the Post Exchange (PX) at Elmendorf for essential gear, I decided to call Jenn. Opting for privacy away from my companions, I stepped outside to a quiet seating area. Eager yet uncertain, I dialed Jenn's number, the anticipation akin to the climb on a rollercoaster's first daunting hill. Pressing send felt like the plunge — it was both thrilling and terrifying. The phone rang endlessly, nearly convincing me I'd be greeted by voicemail, until, at last, a voice said, "Hello?"

"Is Jennifer there?" I inquired.

"Speaking," she replied.

Introducing myself, I mentioned our recent encounter, to which Jenn playfully chided, "Took you long enough to call!" Her response, lighthearted and warm, reignited the ease I'd felt beside her on the flight. Despite the brevity of our conversation, we arranged a hike for the following week.

THE PROMISE OF FOREVER

Our first hike blossomed into dating, affirming what I'd felt from our first encounter: Jenn was destined to be the love of my life. As the holidays neared, and with my deployment to Iraq on the horizon, we discussed how we'd spend the season. Wanting to introduce Jenn to my family, we spent Thanksgiving together in Indiana, a trip that exceeded all expectations and further convinced me she was *the one*. Knowing my rigorous schedule would soon separate us again, our return to Anchorage was accompanied by a deep sadness.

The weeks between Thanksgiving and Christmas whirred by, and although Jenn wouldn't be coming home with me this time, her offer to drive me to the airport underscored the depth of our bond, making our farewell even more difficult. As I passed through security, I glanced back at Jenn, who was waving with the most beautiful smile. I knew it was time to solidify our future.

At home, I broached the topic of marriage with my family, apprehensive about their reaction given my military friend's caution against rushing into marriage. Yet, my family's response was wholly supportive, emboldening me to find the perfect ring. My search led me to an exquisite Irish Claddagh ring. A symbol of love, loyalty, and friendship crafted in Ireland, this ring was a testament to the depth of my commitment to Jenn that was far beyond the superficial allure of opulence. It was unequivocally perfect.

While I should have been more focused on my immediate family and celebrating Christmas with them, I found my thoughts wandering to Jenn. I eagerly counted down the days until I could return to Anchorage, feeling the sting of guilt for not being fully present with my family through my desire to be with Jenn. I knew it would likely be the last Christmas I'd spend with my family before I was deployed, but I felt incomplete without her. Doubts swirled in my mind: Would she accept my proposal? Was I making the right decision? These thoughts chased each other in endless circles until the moment I returned to Anchorage.

My apprehensions persisted until I entered Jenn's living room, where I found her holding a gift for me by the Christmas tree we'd decorated together. Her excited gaze and warm smile dissolved my fears, compelling me to kneel before her. With trembling hands and a quivering voice, I clumsily retrieved a small box from the pouch of my Army hoodie and said, "Never in a million years did I expect to meet the woman of my dreams on a plane, but from the first moment I saw you, I knew you were the one. Will you marry me?" Tears glistened in her eyes as she tried to say "Yes" without crying before sealing our commitment with a kiss that embodied passion and affirmation I'd never felt before. It was one of the very few times I'd felt utterly loved and accepted.

We eagerly dove into wedding planning, prioritizing setting a date before my deployment in the fall of 2006. Jenn's insistence on Saint Patrick's Day initially conflicted with my history of raucous celebrations, but her persistence and our logistic constraints led us to compromise on a St. Patrick's Day wedding. Once we'd decided on our date, the quest for the perfect venue began. Considering that many of our guests would be traveling from afar, we aimed to offer them a unique and unforgettable experience. Alyeska Ski Resort and Spa in Girdwood, Alaska, with its captivating Chapel of Our Lady of the Snows, emerged as our top choice. To confirm availability for March 17, 2006, we planned to visit the resort and chapel in person the next morning.

Our inquiry at Alyeska was met with enthusiasm from an event planner who confirmed our date was available and helped us secure the basics for our event. Next, we visited the chapel, where we were informed that the date was open, but booking required the approval of the managing priest. I explained that despite my Catholic upbringing, we would not need the priest as our plan was to have one of my wife's best friends, Terri, a Methodist Army Chaplain, marry us. Asking if we would still need permission from the priest, she replied, "The priest is the only one who can finalize your booking."

That evening, I received a call from the priest who immediately made inquiries about my Catholic background, sidestepping my questions about the chapel's availability to non-Catholics. After realizing I grew up in the church, he proceeded to deliver a stern warning that marrying outside the Catholic Church would lead to damnation and invalidate our union in God's eyes. His statements momentarily caught me off guard, but I decided not to engage, and instead, I persisted in asking about booking the chapel for March 17th. When the priest realized I wasn't going to engage, the conversation shifted to a business tone, and he ultimately allowed me to reserve the chapel. Although I managed to remain focused during our exchange, the priest's grim prognostication about my spiritual fate lingered with me for far too long.

In the whirlwind of work and wedding preparations, the week of our nuptials approached faster than anticipated. Friends and family, many visiting Alaska for the first time, began to arrive, and despite the relentless demands of work, the excitement was palpable. I navigated through the week on a mix of adrenaline and sleepless anticipation, which only intensified as I stood among my groomsmen, using laughter and a few shots to mask my nerves.

As the ceremony's commencement neared, I positioned myself at the altar next to Terri and fixed my gaze on the far end of the aisle. The bridal party's procession down the aisle was a beautiful sight, but it was Jenn's entrance that captivated me entirely. Dressed in her wedding gown, she radiated a beauty that took my breath away, eliciting an audible gasp from everyone present. As she walked toward me, I struggled to hold back tears, overwhelmed by the thought of spending my life with her. The ceremony itself felt intimate and personal, surrounded by love and laughter, as if it were only Jenn, our pastor, and me in that moment.

Following the ceremony, we gathered all our guests for a group photo before inviting them to commence the St. Patrick's Day celebrations at the Alyeska reception. A horse-drawn carriage awaited to transport hotel guests while Jenn and I seized the moment for photos at the church. Even then, in those quiet moments, I remained in awe of the woman I now called my wife. Our carriage ride to the hotel was a serene journey that we spent wrapped in each other's arms to keep warm against the cold. Stepping out of the carriage and into the hotel as husband and wife ignited a profound realization of my newfound responsibility to protect and love Jenn unconditionally, marking the end of any selfish inclinations.

Our Saint Patrick's Day reception was destined to be an unforgettable celebration, and I relished the opportunity to elevate the party to new heights. The spread of delectable food set the stage, yet it was the green beer, Guinness, and a fully stocked bar that truly set the tone for the evening's merriment and mischief. Living up to my "Frank the Tank" persona I'd adopted during college parties, I was committed to immersing myself in the festivities and constantly sought ways to amplify the night's energy.

As the evening wound down, Jenn and I made our way to our honeymoon suite. When we arrived at our door, I briefly left her outside our room to bid farewell to a groomsman who was catching a red-eye flight, promising her a swift return. When he greeted me, he was holding the small bottle of Jameson Whiskey I'd gifted my groomsmen, and the invitation to finish it before his departure was one I couldn't refuse. Twenty minutes later, the bottle was empty, and I stumbled back to Jenn, considerably more inebriated than when I'd left. Apologizing profusely, I attempted to carry her across the threshold with great ceremony, only to misjudge the distance and accidentally bump her head against the door frame. Jenn, ever the embodiment of coolness and humor, didn't get angry and, instead, laughed it off, her own spirits buoyed by a bit of drunkenness.

For the next two days, we cocooned ourselves in the blissful seclusion of our suite, indulging in nothing more strenuous than eating, watching movies, sleeping, and loving each other. Those two days were among the happiest of my life, a cherished memory filled with laughter, love, and the simple joy of being together.

Chapter **3**

RUNNING AWAY

AFTER OUR WEDDING, we only had a few days of celebration before my impending return to work. The preparation for
Operation Iraqi Freedom was ramping up, which meant
I had a non-stop schedule of training exercises until my
block leave in July, when Jenn and I would go on a proper
honeymoon. Amid this whirlwind, Jenn and I cherished
the moments we could steal together, understanding that
my impending deployments — to Fairbanks for field training, followed by Thailand for Cobra Gold 2006 — meant
our time together would be scarce. This cycle of training
and fleeting reunions gave the early days of our marriage
a sense of longing and appreciation that kept the flame of
our newlywed phase alive longer than most.

When July rolled around, I was buzzing with excitement
about our honeymoon, especially since we'd decided to visit Hawaii and stay at the Hilton Hawaiian Village right on
the famous Waikiki Beach. I'd spent the early 2000s living,
working, and going to school in Hawaii, so the thrill of this
trip was twofold for me. Not only would we be enjoying our

honeymoon, but I'd also get to share that part of my life with Jenn. Maybe it was because we met on a plane, but traveling together always felt right. We'd splurged on first-class seats, and, finding ourselves alone in our aisle, we immersed ourselves in movies and indulged in the surprisingly good food offered by Delta. At just over three months pregnant, our little family was headed to one of my most cherished places in the world, second only to Yellowstone National Park.

That week in Hawaii, we embraced every adventure the island had to offer. I got sunburned, as was tradition, and we watched fireworks, attended a luau, explored an aquarium, and went snorkeling. All too soon, it was time to leave Hawaii and head for our next destination: South Bend, Indiana. We were returning to my hometown to introduce Jenn to all my family and friends who hadn't been able to make it to Alaska for our wedding. This trip also gave me a chance to spend time with my family one last time before my deployment to Iraq.

I was particularly excited about visiting my mom at the OBGYN office where she worked. They'd planned to do an ultrasound so my mom could see her first grandchild, David, for the first time. During the ultrasound, I noticed a change in the technician's expression. A glance at my mom confirmed she'd noticed it too, despite her effort to remain composed. I felt a sinking feeling growing inside me. Jenn also saw the change and shared a look that conveyed a silent acknowledgement of our shared worry.

The silence seemed to stretch on forever before the technician and my mom finally began to share their observations. David wasn't growing at the expected rate, and there were other signs that raised red flags. My mom fetched the OBGYN, Dr. G, who entered with a lightness in his step and cracked a few dad jokes before turning semi-serious.

"This isn't something to worry about too much right now," he assured us. "See your doctor when you get back home. It could be a simple mix-up in dates. Don't worry until you've seen your doctor." His calm demeanor and honest approach gave Jenn and me a sliver of hope that perhaps the situation wasn't as dire as it seemed. We tried to push our worries to the back of our minds, determined to enjoy the rest of our visit in South Bend and soak up time with loved ones.

Upon our return to Anchorage, the brief respite I found from the uncertainty of David's condition was quickly overtaken by the relentless pace of deployment preparations. My days were consumed by the necessity to pack equipment, complete airborne jumps, meet physical fitness standards, and engage in continuous training exercises. My unit's leadership played a crucial role in arranging my schedule so I could accompany Jenn to the critical appointments for David. Their understanding underscored the gravity of our situation and offered a bit of solace.

At our first follow-up appointment back home, our OBGYN confirmed our worst fears: David's development was not progressing as it should. The news felt like a physical blow as if the very air had been sucked from my lungs, leaving me grappling with an intense emotion I had never experienced before. Jenn, too, was visibly shaken, her tears a silent testament to our shared anguish. I struggled to maintain composure and find the strength to inquire about our next steps. Our doctor, a beacon of compassion amid our storm of despair, advised us to take things one step at a time, starting with an amniocentesis to identify the cause of David's slow development. This procedure, she explained, would involve carefully inserting a needle into the placenta under ultrasound guidance to collect amniotic fluid for testing.

THE SEA OF UNCERTAINTY

The week and a half leading up to the test was a blur of anxiety and anticipation. The familiar setting of the ultrasound room, now cast in a dim, somber light, took on a more foreboding feeling as we prepared for the procedure. The sight of the needle, so skinny and long, sent a wave of panic through me. Jenn gripped my hand tight with fear, and for the first time, I felt a profound sense of helplessness. My upbringing in an Irish Catholic family had taught me to mask vulnerability with anger or frustration, but facing Jenn's pain, I knew what she needed most was my presence and support.

As we walked back to her car, I wrapped her in a hug, trying to convey every ounce of love and reassurance I could muster. "I love you more than there are stars in the sky," I whispered, a promise of my unwavering support. Yet, as I got into my truck and started to drive away, I saw Jenn in her car with her head hung low and tears running down her face. Unfortunately, the military's hold over my schedule meant I couldn't simply follow my heart's desire to abandon everything and comfort her. Torn between my instincts and obligations, I told myself I had no choice, that the Army dictated my time, not me. This wasn't the time to fall apart, I reassured myself. She'd be okay. We'd be okay. I began compartmentalizing the experience to push away the fear and uncertainty that threatened to overwhelm me.

Seventy-two hours felt like an eternity as we waited for our test results. Sitting in the waiting room again, nerves frayed and hearts heavy, I found myself grappling with how to support Jenn and make her feel loved in this sea of uncertainty. Despite my never-ending stream of thoughts, my struggle to express my empathy and compassion for Jenn made me feel inadequate. When we were called to the exam room, I held Jenn's hand in a silent promise of togetherness, no matter what the news.

Our doctor broke the heavy silence with a diagnosis that seemed to echo around the room: Trisomy 18, a genetic disorder that threatened our son's very chance at life. She explained the complexities and risks, each word landing with the weight of the world. Frozen in place, I barely breathed as Jenn's tears began to fall. The reality that our son would likely not survive was a blow like no other.

Further explanations about the risks to Jenn's health and the tough decisions ahead felt like navigating a minefield blindfolded. Our doctor's discomfort in delivering such news was clear, yet her professionalism in outlining our options provided a grim sort of clarity. Stunned, we left her office, not with answers but with a heavy burden of choices neither of us felt prepared to make. Seeking solace in the familiar, we found ourselves at the bagel shop we'd often visited after appointments. There, the pressing need to find solutions and understanding led me to suggest reaching out to my mom and her doctor's office for more insight into Trisomy 18. Jenn's smile reassured me that we were in this together.

My call to my mom revealed the depth of our shared pain, her disappointment tangible through the phone. Yet, it was through her that we found a glimmer of hope. She suggested that my cousin Fernando, a pediatric specialist, could offer the guidance we so desperately needed. The prospect of speaking with someone who could provide clear, honest answers about what lay ahead for David was a lifeline to cling to. However, arranging a visit to Fernando's hospital in Indianapolis presented its own set of logistic challenges, especially with my impending deployment to Iraq. The weight of the decision we faced — to pursue every possible option for David's care or confront the possibility of saying goodbye — was overwhelming. I was again torn between my duties and the personal crisis that was threatening to consume us.

In the end, the decision to inform my leadership about the Trisomy 18 diagnosis and the need for emergency leave was driven by the stark realization that time with David was the most precious commodity we had. Their support, particularly from individuals I'd braced myself to battle for understanding, was unexpected and invaluable, reinforcing the notion that in the darkest times, clarity often comes from where we least expect it.

Within a day, we found ourselves on a Delta Airlines flight to Indianapolis, Indiana. Exhaustion was our constant companion, not just from the travel but also from the emotional weight we were carrying. Our time in Indianapolis was brief but invaluable. Meeting with Fernando, whose insights into Trisomy 18 came from years of experience, shed light on our situation in ways we hadn't anticipated. He presented a perspective that lifted some of the weight off our shoulders: the risks to Jenn, while present, hadn't yet materialized, tipping the odds in our favor that they might not manifest at all.

This meeting gave us the information we needed to decide about David's life. The clarity and peace we gained from our discussion with Fernando solidified our belief that this was not our decision but God's. It was with much lighter hearts that we boarded our flight back to Alaska, carrying with us a sense of resolution and a newfound strength to face whatever lay ahead together.

INTROSPECTION AND APPREHENSION

In the whirlwind of David's health concerns and the intensity of deployment preparations, time seemed to slip away. Before I could fully grasp the weight of each passing day, October 10, 2006, dawned — deployment day had arrived. That morning, in the quiet of our home, I found myself reflecting on the journey Jenn and I had embarked upon together. When she asked if I was ready, I gave a silent nod, a simple gesture belying the storm of emotions within.

A CD filled with our favorite songs for the drive to the base was a small token of the life we shared, a life now paused by the call of duty. The unexpected news of my delayed flight gifted us with a few more precious hours together, and we spent the time sharing a meal at the PX and wandering its aisles.

Back in the truck and driven by a spontaneous desire to cherish our remaining moments, I steered us down a secluded path on base that only I knew about. It was there, in the beauty of Alaska's backcountry, that Jenn and I shared one last romp in the hay. It was one of the most intense experiences I've had with another person, and it was also one last chance to hold her close before facing the uncertainties ahead. This intimate moment, set against the backdrop of the quiet forest, was a poignant testament to the depth of our connection. It was spontaneous, adventurous, and filled with an intensity that momentarily lifted the weight of our reality.

Arriving back at the Command Post with only minutes to spare, our goodbye was a fleeting embrace that had to last us through the coming months apart. As I boarded the bus, the physical distance that began to unfold between us felt like a widening chasm, filled with unspoken fears and uncertainties. The journey to Kuwait was a blur of introspection and apprehension, and when I stepped off the plane, I was met with a wave of heat, a harsh welcome that mirrored the internal heat of my anxiety and dread.

Moments after my boots hit the ground at Camp Buehring, I received an emergency Red Cross message telling me to return home because David had died. As I prepared to face the unimaginable, I felt a mix of dread and an urgent need to be with Jenn for the stillbirth so I could support her through the intense grief of losing our son.

Holding David in the hospital and feeling the weight of his stillness was a moment of profound sorrow and love, an indelible memory I knew would forever mark our hearts. The days that followed were filled with funeral arrangements and quiet mourning. Jenn told me that the night I'd left, she'd had a dream that David had died. The next day, at her weekly ultrasound, the doctor couldn't find David's heartbeat, and he wasn't moving. After a number of tests, she'd told Jenn that David had passed.

Because of the depth of our loss, my battalion gave me the option to remain home for six months. The idea of not returning to the battlefield was a fleeting temptation, but the fear of my emotional ineptness and the harm that it may cause Jenn, my marriage, and our future together was overwhelming, so I decided to return to Iraq. I tried to rationalize my decision by making myself sound more important to my platoon than I was so I could justify my decision to leave.

I knew I wasn't going back for noble reasons; I was going back because I was a coward. The thought of having to confront all the emotions I was feeling, as well as be a support system for Jenn, scared me a thousand times more than a war zone did. I managed trauma with anger, and I didn't want to be angry toward Jenn because I knew what she needed was love, compassion, empathy, and time — all things that felt foreign to me and that I knew I couldn't provide in the moment.

Looking back, it was this decision that set the tone for how we would deal with trauma as a married couple. We'd separate, process alone, and then meet back up down the road. While separating yourself from your spouse in times of intense struggle might sound ideal to some people, it isolates you and robs you of the opportunity to grow through the trauma together. I try not to have regrets in life because it's often the decisions people regret

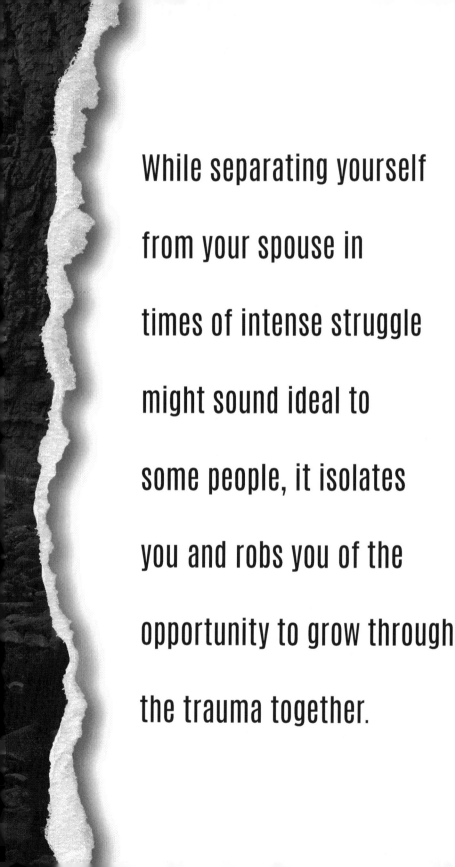

While separating yourself

from your spouse in

times of intense struggle

might sound ideal to

some people, it isolates

you and robs you of the

opportunity to grow through

the trauma together.

that provide the most education and change in life, but looking back, I would wholeheartedly do things differently. The emotional turmoil of our goodbye as I returned to an active war zone and the image of Jenn's tear-stained face haunted me throughout my journey back to Kuwait and still does to this day.

Chapter 4

DANCING WITH DEATH

SADNESS, CONFUSION, AND loneliness fought for attention next to the anger I felt toward God for taking David. The belief system I was raised in, which promised protection and love from a benevolent God for the good and well-meaning, began to crumble under the weight of my grief. While I didn't doubt His existence, my faith in His benevolence and my place within His grace began to waver.

When my flight landed in Kuwait, I headed through the security checkpoint, where I was relieved to see US Army personnel waiting. I approached a sergeant, introduced myself, and despite not being on his list, I was able to show my ID and secure a ride to Camp Buehring. Upon arrival, I retrieved my ballistic helmet, Kevlar vest, and other personal protective items before heading to check-in.

The administrative sergeant was puzzled by my unexpected arrival, assuming I had opted to stay home with Jenn. Once he reviewed my paperwork, he realized I hadn't completed training before returning to Alaska to be with Jenn, a fact that prevented me from reuniting with my platoon. However, overhearing talk of a helicopter bound for Baghdad International Airport, I saw my opportunity. Instead of staying at Camp Buehring to complete my training, I discreetly inquired about the flight, and soon I was on my way to Baghdad.

Landing in Baghdad, I once again had to explain my presence, this time to a First Sergeant who wanted to know how I'd managed to board the helicopter. My eager explanation led to an amusing exchange, but it was clear I was still far from joining my platoon. Directed to temporary billet housing, I found myself near the 172nd Stryker Brigade, our sister brigade in Alaska, which had been in Baghdad for more than a year. With time on my hands, I sought their advice, hoping to better prepare myself for the challenges ahead. However, instead of getting tactical advice, I learned how war changes you and beats your soul into the ground. *Not me,* I thought. *That won't happen to me.*

After a few days of hanging out at the base, I received news that I was scheduled for a helicopter flight that night to join my platoon at FOB Kalsu. Before long, I found myself awaiting the arrival of the Blackhawk that would transport me to the front. In the air, the darkness was pervasive, pierced only by sporadic gunfire, explosions, and flares illuminating parts of the night sky. It was a stark reminder of the reality I was stepping into, and relief washed over me when we landed safely. Collecting my bag, I made my way into the main area of the FOB, where I ran into Dustin, a friend from my platoon. His surprise at seeing me was evident in his wide eyes and open mouth as he exclaimed, "What the fuck are you doing here?"

I simply replied, "It was time to get back to work, brother," and followed him to our platoon's temporary quarters. He pointed out the essentials — chow hall, PX, gym — as we walked. The tent was buzzing with activity as everyone was returning from a mission, and their warm reception, filled with smiles and laughter, immediately put me at ease. Notably, no one mentioned Jenn or David, a silence I found comforting.

OUTSIDE THE WIRE

The very next morning, I was introduced to our area of responsibility in Iraq. The learning curve was steep and demanded quick adaptation. That day's mission proceeded without incident, and shortly after returning to the FOB, we were briefed on a nighttime mission, which set the relentless pace of our operations. Listening to *Many Men* by 50 Cent became a ritual that helped me to mentally prepare for the realities of the mission ahead. This song underscored the harsh truth that anyone without an American flag on their shoulder was a potential threat.

We set out as night fell, the eerie quiet of the mission a sharp contrast to the intensity of our preparation. However, during our return to base, the Humvee I was driving struck an IED. Thankfully, the ground absorbed much of the explosion, minimizing damage to the Humvee and sparing us from serious injury, though the shock of the blast left me disoriented. In those moments and the immediate aftermath, my focus, like that of all the members of my platoon, was solely on the mission.

Our training to suppress fear and rise above the chaos allowed us to apprehend the individual responsible for the attack. That night was a testament to the solidarity and readiness of our platoon. The swift, coordinated response, driven not by fear but by a commitment to each other, was unlike anything I'd experienced before. After successfully concluding the mission and handing the prisoner over to the Iraqi authorities, we returned to our portion of the base at Kalsu.

The debriefing session and assessment of the Humvee's damage took place amid an atmosphere of camaraderie and relief. Everyone was visibly proud of their performance, and even though not everyone always got along on a personal level, in that moment, the unity of our platoon resembled that of a team who'd just won the Super Bowl. With the remnants of the day's adrenaline still coursing through me and my head still ringing from the blast, I was starkly reminded of my mortality. The vivid memory of Jenn's tearful farewell played on a loop in my mind, underscoring the harsh reality that I might not return home. The thought of leaving her without expressing the depth of my love felt intolerable.

Compelled by this realization, I resolved to leave behind something for Jenn, a tangible piece of my heart she could cling to in my absence. That night, I faced my fears of putting my feelings down on paper head-on and poured my soul into the sincerest letter I'd ever written, detailing how her presence had fundamentally changed me for the better. Sealing the letter, I inscribed the envelope with instructions to ensure its delivery to Jenn should the worst happen before placing it securely in my footlocker.

ROUTE CHICAGO

Life in Iraq was a blend of tranquility and sudden intensity. For the most part, our sector was relatively peaceful, allowing us moments of calm amid the chaos of war. However, this semblance of calm was disrupted by the news that we were to relocate to Camp Fallujah. Tasked with providing security to the notoriously dangerous Karmah, Iraq, the briefing room was silent as we absorbed the gravity of our new assignment. The move to Camp Fallujah indicated a significant escalation in danger and the likelihood of extreme loss.

Upon arrival in Karmah, our platoon was divided to provide maximum coverage. I was attached to Squad One and was stationed with the Iraqi police on Route Chicago, an infamous road known for its deadly IEDs. Our stint at the police station was fraught with tension and uncertainty as we lived in close quarters with individuals whose loyalties were ambiguous at best. Despite the constant threat, we gradually managed to improve our strategic position in the area, eventually allowing our platoon to relocate back to Camp Fallujah in an area we named Camp Geronimo. This move offered improved living and operational conditions and a rare opportunity for rest and recuperation.

Though we'd experienced a brief respite from the relentless pace of work during our transition into Camp Geronimo, we'd switched from night to day operations, and the tension was evident on everyone's faces. Operating under the veil of night had been our ally, shielding us from the heightened dangers of daylight. Yet, on Valentine's Day 2007, we were once again thrust into the broad daylight of Iraq's perilous terrain along Route Chicago. During the drive, I had a sudden, unexplainable urge to combat-lock my door, a practice I normally avoided due to its potential hazards in a rollover scenario.

Only a short distance down Route Chicago, an IED detonated directly under the driver-side door of our Humvee. I was momentarily knocked unconscious, and as I came to, I saw my door had been blown open by the force of the explosion and posed an immediate threat to my exposed side. I grappled with the door, securing it shut to shield myself as I attempted to continue driving. The Humvee eventually came to a halt, its engine dead from the blast.

Our team swiftly secured the perimeter, adhering to our training in the immediate aftermath of an attack. The damaged vehicle was towed back to the Iraqi police station, and, despite the chaos, a deep sense of gratitude permeated my thoughts as I reflected on the craftsmanship of the Humvee, its origins tracing back to my hometown in South Bend, Indiana. The vehicle had offered me protection in a moment of critical vulnerability, and I wondered if my friends working in the plant would ever truly know how many lives they'd saved, including my own.

Although I was thankful to have survived, my body was wracked by a pounding headache, an overwhelming sense of nausea, and a profound disorientation. I struggled to process the event, to articulate thoughts, or to foresee a path forward from the shock. For those reasons, I was sent back to Camp Geronimo to get medical attention and rest.

When I arrived back at Camp Geronimo, I went to the call center and reached out to Jenn. I sought the comfort of her voice yet found myself unable to convey the depth of my experience. I desperately wanted to share what had happened to me in detail, but I was stopped by an overwhelming need to shield her from the reality of my world. Ever my anchor in a tumultuous sea, I yearned to be reunited with Jenn during my upcoming leave. Even though I was fearful about how she would react to the physical toll recent events had on me physically and mentally, I knew she would show patience and empathy, as always.

RETURN TO KALSU

By April 2007, I found myself back in Baghdad watching TV in the chow hall, only to be blindsided by a CNN report announcing that our tour of duty had been extended. This revelation ignited a torrent of anger and frustration and a newfound sense of vulnerability. The extension of my deployment felt like a betrayal, amplifying my fear of not returning home. This moment marked a shift in my perspective on combat, and the mission transformed from one of strategic objectives to a singular focus on survival. Propelled by a mix of anger and determination, my allegiance to my comrades intensified.

In the months that followed, the rhythm of loss became a haunting melody of farewells to fallen comrades. The high operational tempo continued to isolate me from Jenn, leaving me to grapple with a growing resignation to accept my mortality. I resolved to confront death head-on, channeling my anger into the war happening around and in me. This grim acceptance became my armor, distancing me from the remnants of who I once was. My love for photography,

In the months that

followed, the rhythm of

loss became a haunting

melody of farewells to

fallen comrades.

correspondence, and the very essence of my connection to home and to Jenn all fell by the wayside. Engulfed by a warrior's rage, nothing else mattered but the mission and the survival of those who bore the American flag alongside me.

A few months later, and after largely freeing Karmah from the terrorism that plagued it, my platoon was sent back to FOB Kalsu. Upon arrival, it was evident that the environment had become hostile. Iranian-backed militias frequently targeted our base, challenging our presence. As the confrontations continued, our platoon was one of several tasked with tracking down the cells firing Katyusha rockets at the base. One morning, after an extended mission, we returned with just enough time to catch breakfast at the chow hall. Hungry and tired, we quickly grabbed our food. My friend Brent and I chose a spot away from the others, engrossed in the news as we ate.

Finishing our meal and walking toward the exit, the first rocket struck the chow hall. The explosion knocked us to the ground, disorienting us amid the chaos. As we regained our senses, I looked at Brent's face, and, without thinking, we both ran back into the smoke, where we found civilian cooks, some struggling because of their injuries, while others struggled to maintain their bearings while running to find the exit, so we helped. Just as we safely evacuated the last civilian, another rocket hit.

As I began to set up a casualty collection point for the civilians, Brent broke cover under a rocket attack to regroup with our guys who'd been eating on the other side of the chow hall. We feared the worst because it looked like the rocket had hit right where they'd been sitting, but we hadn't seen any of them as we evacuated the civilians.

Fortunately, the rest of our team had also left their table right before the first rocket landed, and because of that, the injuries they'd sustained were not life-threatening, allowing for local treatment and quick recovery. This experience highlighted the thin line between life and death, a reality shaped by the narrowest margins.

The rocket explosions worsened my headaches, making it hard for me to find the right words or form complete sentences. To compensate, I often swore to fill the gaps, a technique that worked surprisingly well. My brothers understood me perfectly. The profound camaraderie in the military is an understanding beyond words, unmatched by any other relationship in my life.

Following the rocket attack, our mission to find those responsible intensified, and our operational pace increased. I thrived on the busyness as I preferred being on missions and staying active to waiting in anticipation of the next attack. Time flew by, and suddenly, it was October. Despite my efforts, I couldn't shake my thoughts about David. I still harbored deep anger toward God and questioned Him about the suffering in the world. These silent accusations were met with no response, which only fueled my anger. However, I convinced myself that this anger was not negative but necessary. It was the drive I needed to fulfill my purpose in Iraq and ensure my survival so I could return home.

THE FINAL MISSION

The final months of my deployment merged into a blur, and I consciously tempered any excitement about our upcoming

The profound

camaraderie in

the military is an

understanding beyond

words, unmatched by

any other relationship

in my life.

departure. Too often, I'd seen the joy of the impending end of deployment cut tragically short. This awareness, fueled by my deep-seated anger, kept my focus sharp.

My final mission took us near Iskandariya, Iraq. The night operation was proceeding flawlessly, yet an unsettling feeling gnawed at me like the one I'd experienced before being hit by the IED on Route Chicago. As we were returning to base, our Humvee was struck by an EFP capable of piercing through 10 inches of armor. The impact was devastating, nearly flipping our vehicle and causing the most severe impact I'd experienced yet.

Fortunately, moments before the blast, our gunner had leaned down to share his thoughts on a conversation the platoon leader and I were having, a move that miraculously spared his life. The convoy halted immediately, and our team secured the perimeter before searching for the assailant. My platoon sergeant, Brent, hurried to our Humvee. When he saw me, he said, "You look like you just took a huge bong rip." His assessment reflected the disorientation we all felt. That night, three of us were sent back to FOB Kalsu for medical attention, and within a day, our platoon identified the attackers. Shockingly, we'd discovered they were the very Iraqi police officers we'd been working with.

After receiving medical attention for obvious physical injuries, I continued to maintain the facade that I was ready for action. Even though I was still struggling with processing my thoughts and speaking, everyone believed I was physically fit to continue. In reality, my vision was plagued with dots, purple flares, and persistent stars, making my world unrecognizable. My memory faltered, and my temper flared unpredictably. My body now felt alien.

THE JOURNEY HOME

A few weeks after my last mission, I began my journey home from Iraq. The first stop was Baghdad International Airport, where I embarked on a personal mission to reunite with my father, a former Charlie Company Ranger, LRRP, during Vietnam. He'd been contracted by Hill International to help oversee the reconstruction of healthcare facilities in Iraq and was living in the Green Zone. We successfully arranged a meeting, and when I saw him, I felt like a vulnerable child longing for their dad's comfort and wanted to run into his arms.

Suppressing my emotions, I greeted him with a facade of toughness, jokingly welcoming him to the chaos of Iraq. He laughed, and we spent the next hour or so dining at the Air Force chow hall, sharing a profoundly special moment without delving into the war's harrowing realities. However, his knowing look revealed his recognition of my transformation, a change only a fellow warrior could comprehend.

After exchanging our goodbyes, I boarded my flight to Kuwait. The next leg of the journey back to Alaska included a layover in Ireland, a place of my heritage I'd always dreamed of visiting. Despite my dislike for window seats, I'd eagerly chosen one for this flight, hoping to see if Ireland was as green as its fame suggested. Having now seen the country for myself, I can confirm the view was amazing. During our layover, I wandered into a jewelry store, and my thoughts turned to Jenn as I spotted a beautiful white-gold Celtic cross with a deep green emerald in the middle made by Shanore, the same company that created her wedding ring. Feeling a deep connection to the piece, I bought it.

Landing at Elmendorf Air Force Base in Anchorage we turned in our weapons and gear and boarded the buses to Fort Richardson. The sight of friends and family waiting to greet us was overwhelming, especially considering my most recent brush with death in Iraq. The joy of being home, of reuniting with Jenn, was immense, yet I pushed down the whirlwind of emotions and thoughts, unable to articulate my feelings.

Once cleared to leave, Jenn and I headed home, looking forward to some quiet time together. However, despite the comfort of being with Jenn, sleep eluded me. The first forty-eight hours passed without a wink of rest, and by the third day, the exhaustion was overwhelming. The only time I was able to sleep was the few hours after my daily PT run from the base to Fort Richardson National Cemetery to visit David. It was there, in the snow-covered grounds of the memorial site, that I found the peace I needed to bring my mind and body to rest upon my return.

Not only was I struggling to sleep, but my emotions were constantly frayed. After being home for a few months, I had an encounter with a neighbor over our privacy fence and they made a casual observation about how good our new TV looked through our windows. This statement felt like an intrusion, and my confrontational response to this incident and others revealed more than just irritation; it laid bare the profound internal conflicts I grappled with that evoked the same fight-or-flight response I experienced in active combat.

Those experiences, particularly the ones revealing my unresolved anger and the way I managed conflict, highlighted a disconnect not just with my environment but within myself. Not only did I yearn for space and privacy, but I also wanted peace and autonomy. Acknowledging this, Jenn and I began to dream of a different life, one where open space and the freedom to grow as a family could offer us the healing and unity we desperately sought.

Our search for a new home led us to a place that felt like destiny calling. Overlooking breathtaking Alaskan vistas, the house we discovered was not just a dwelling but a promise of new beginnings. The builder and his wife became close allies, and I learned valuable lessons in communication, patience, and the importance of aligning with those who truly understood our needs.

As we worked on purchasing our new home, I returned to Fort Richardson for a mandatory post-deployment health assessment. This procedure, designed in response to growing concerns about traumatic brain injuries and the perceived neglect by the Department of Defense, was more serious than I initially realized. I approached the assessment with the intent to avoid any red flags, especially regarding traumatic brain injuries and post-traumatic stress. However, my request for medication to alleviate migraines and improve sleep inadvertently revealed more than I'd intended. Despite my efforts to conceal my struggles, my assessments indicated significant concerns.

The outcomes of these evaluations heralded the end of my career in the infantry. I was transferred to the Warrior Transition Unit for specialized care — a move I was internally resistant to but ultimately recognized as necessary. Despite the official optimism about my recovery, I was acutely aware that my days as an infantryman were over.

Many appointments and consultations later, my neurologist confirmed my fears: I could not return to the infantry or engage in high-risk activities like parachuting. The risk of further brain injury was too great, a reality I struggled to accept. This news only fueled my anger and frustration. Already known as "Grandpa" in my platoon for being the oldest member, I soon adopted the moniker of "Angry Grandpa" at the Warrior Transition Unit. While I tried to maintain a facade of cool detachment, I grappled with fear and uncertainty about my future and how I would support my family.

Faced with limited options for remaining in the military, I was directed toward a finance role, an option that felt misaligned with my identity as an infantryman. I knew they wouldn't have wanted me any more than I wanted them, so instead, I chose retirement from the US Army and a return to construction management, the field I'd studied in college and a trade I knew well from working with my dad in the late 90s and early 2000s. On February 26, 2009, I retired as Sergeant Eric Donoho, grappling with the transition and the profound changes it implied for my life and identity.

The farewell party for my platoon, set against the backdrop of our new home, was a bittersweet celebration of camaraderie and change. It served as a poignant reminder of the bonds formed in the crucible of service, even as we faced the inevitability of moving on. In the aftermath, I clung to the belief that those bonds would be unchanged even as I transitioned into civilian life, a comforting lie that masked the deeper truth of isolation and the end of an era.

Chapter 5

DEAL WITH GOD

THE ABRUPT END to my military career was not followed by a gentle transition into civilian life. Everyone around me seemed to be saying, "Don't worry, Eric, life will be amazing in retirement without the weight of military responsibilities. You'll have time to decompress, to relax!" But, if anything, life's perpetual motion seemed to accelerate, and the stress and trauma I'd accumulated over the years were a constant noise in my mind.

During the process of getting ready for a vacation, we experienced our first post-retirement crisis when Jenn's Achilles tendon snapped during a routine workout. Throughout her surgery and painstaking recovery process, I found unexpected solace in crisis management, my military training rendering me a steadfast pillar of support.

As we navigated the aftermath of my wife's injury, she became pregnant again, and the flicker of joy we felt became a beacon of hope. Yet, beneath our shared excitement and my renewed sense of purpose, there was a current of unease. Painful memories of David continued to rise to the surface, tainting our joy, making every day a struggle. Not long into the pregnancy, a cruel twist of fate led to a miscarriage. Witnessing my wife's profound grief, I was once again engulfed in anger. This time, my fury found a singular target: God. I was haunted by my need to understand. "Why, God?" became an accusation, a challenge to the fairness of our trials.

While navigating our latest loss, my wife discovered a lump in her right breast. My initial reaction was paralysis, a numbing inability to process yet another potential blow to our family's well-being. As my wife voiced her concerns and sought comfort, I was ensnared in a silent confrontation with my own demons, my anger boiling over into a silent scream directed at a seemingly indifferent deity.

Several days after her initial discovery, Jenn had her biopsy. When she returned home, it was clear from our conversation that my presence at the biopsy would have been meaningful to her — something I hadn't considered prior to her appointment. I realized I'd missed an opportunity to support her in a way she needed so we could navigate our shared grief and fear constructively. This revelation weighed heavily on me. In my eagerness to comfort her with an embrace, I forgot about the physical pain she was enduring from the procedure, a misstep that symbolized my broader failures.

Three days later, Jenn received a call from her doctor requesting an immediate appointment. This time, she asked me to accompany her. Sitting together in the doctor's office, we learned that what was initially dismissed as benign was, in fact, a rare cancer known as a phyllodes tumor. The doctor informed us that the knowledge and treatment options for this type of cancer were still developing, and seeking a specialist outside of Alaska was essential. The gravity of the situation mirrored the helplessness we felt during our previous trials, yet, holding hands, we knew we had each other.

Rooted in suppression and diversion, my approach to coping proved increasingly ineffective, eroding the foundations of our relationship. Acknowledging this pattern was a painful recognition of the vast chasm between the person I wanted to be for Jenn and the person I was. My struggle to articulate my feelings, to bridge the gap between my internal chaos and the support my wife deserved, left me feeling isolated and ineffectual. This disconnect only fueled my frustration, trapping me in a cycle of anger that drained the joy from our lives.

In response to her diagnosis, Jenn and I sought solace at our home on Bear Mountain, a place that offered us refuge and breathtaking views of the natural beauty surrounding us. It was there, in the quiet of our living room, that I recognized the need for a change in how I supported Jenn. Determined to be present for her, I consulted my doctor about managing my own anxiety, a step toward becoming the partner Jenn needed as she navigated her cancer journey. Admitting my struggles and seeking help marked a pivotal moment in my personal growth.

A SENSE OF ACCOMPLISHMENT

Jenn and I decided on treatment at Cedars-Sinai in Los Angeles, where we were confronted with the harsh reality that a full mastectomy of Jenn's right breast was necessary due to the way the biopsy was performed. We hadn't expected this news, and once again, we both retreated into ourselves, not speaking, not sure what to do. Jenn was now faced with making a choice between a long-term reconstruction process of her breast or an innovative, eight-hour surgery that would use her latissimus dorsi muscle to support a new breast. Jenn opted for the latter.

In the few weeks we had to ourselves before Jenn's surgery, we decided to pursue a shared dream of visiting the overwater bungalows in the French Polynesian islands. I threw myself into planning both our dream vacation and the logistics for our stay in Los Angeles post-surgery, a task I navigated with a determination that allowed me a moment of pride amid the turmoil. My efforts to be present for Jenn during this time gave me a sense of accomplishment. And after returning to LA for a quick pre-surgery checkup, we embarked on our journey from LAX to Bora Bora, flying business class to the Saint Regis, a resort made famous by the movie *Couples Retreat*.

The timing for our getaway was perfect. Arriving in a tranquil period between travel seasons lent a sense of solitude to our stay. Initially booked into an overwater bungalow with a hot tub, the staff, upon learning of our situation, graciously upgraded us to a more luxurious bungalow with a pool — the very one featured in the movie. This setting was the epitome of exotic beauty. It was a place where reality seemed to bend around the edges, enveloping us in its serene embrace.

Each day began with breakfast on the deck overlooking the tranquil ocean and ended with dinners by the water.

Activities like jet ski rides and snorkeling filled our days, creating an atmosphere of carefree joy. But despite the reprieve, both Jenn and I were wrestling with thoughts about the future. Jenn, much like me, put on a brave face, but I knew her concerns about what lay ahead were never far from her mind. Despite my understanding of her fears, I found myself unable to open up about my own, a barrier that kept us from fully sharing our burdens.

As our time in paradise neared its end, Jenn expressed a longing to return home to be surrounded by the familiar comforts of our life in Alaska before her surgery. Seizing this opportunity to fulfill her wish, I leveraged all my resources to rearrange our travel plans from the other side of the globe, a gesture that, for once, allowed me to alleviate some of her stress and make a tangible difference in her journey. This act of service was a rare win for me in my efforts to support Jenn.

After spending a few days back home in Alaska, we returned to Los Angeles for Jenn's surgery. Trying to be understanding of our family's expectations and emotions while suppressing my own compounded the stress of the day. However, the relief that washed over me when we learned the surgery was successful cannot be overstated. It was a major hurdle overcome, a momentary pause in the relentless march of our challenges. The recovery period that followed was intense and filled with appointments and milestones, but eventually, Jenn was given a triumphant all-clear from cancer.

Life after cancer morphed into a complex battle for me, especially in the silence where my struggles intensified. Seeking solace and a means to quiet the inner turmoil, I turned back to the mountains, immersing myself in climbing and earning my civilian mountaineering certification. The Alaskan ranges became the refuge where I could orchestrate climbs with friends and embrace the busyness that kept my darker thoughts at bay. Meanwhile, Jenn channeled her post-cancer resilience into a pursuit of greater fulfillment in her career. Her ambition led to a significant advancement, propelling us toward a new chapter in Washington, DC. This move, we hoped, would be the fresh start needed to redefine ourselves after enduring such profound upheaval.

JOY AND ANTICIPATION

Although we hadn't sold our dream home in Alaska, in the summer of 2010, Jenn and I locked the doors, said farewell, and embraced the promise of new beginnings in the capital. Our prior visits had culminated in securing a residence in Arlington in a charming yet unassuming house on 7th St. Despite its disarray during our initial viewing — attributable to the owners' young family — my wariness was piqued upon learning of their Middle Eastern heritage. Wrestling with my biases, I questioned whether my suspicions were a byproduct of my service in Iraq or genuinely instinctual. Striving to override what I feared was prejudice, I reminded myself of the importance of trust, especially in legal agreements bound by American law.

However, the reality that awaited us was wildly different from our expectations. The house was in disarray, with uncleaned carpets, damaged walls, and an infestation of black mold pervading every corner. Faced with this dire situation, we found ourselves ensnared in a legal battle to vacate the premises, hindered further by a clause in the Virginia Landlord Tenant Act that left us unprotected due to the fine print in our lease.

This episode in DC exacerbated my struggle to assimilate to civilian life and the dense population and cultural diversity added layers of complexity to my adjustment. Our efforts to secure a safe living environment drained us emotionally, culminating in the discovery of a peaceful haven in Waynewood, courtesy of the kindest landlords we'd encountered in the city. Despite their warmth and empathy, my pervasive anger cast a shadow over this period, transforming our new home into a personal prison as I grappled with my unease at living in an area that was such a target for terrorists, fear of being unable to protect Jenn, and unresolved emotions resulting from my transition out of the military.

After finally settling in, we invited our friends from Alaska, who were now living in Ohio, to spend Halloween weekend with us. During the festivities, Jenn emerged from the hallway, a look of excitement spread across her face, and said, "Eric, we're pregnant." This was our fifth attempt at starting a family, and I was immediately filled with a mix of elation and trepidation. Determined not to dampen Jenn's spirits, I adopted a state of supportive optimism so we could experience a moment of joy with some of our closest friends.

That night, we ventured out to celebrate, and I embodied my "Frank the Tank" persona with unparalleled precision. The evening's festivities concluded on our back deck, where the physical and emotional toll of the night culminated in a solitary moment of reflection and a profound conversation with God. It was there, amid my drunken vulnerability, that I made a vow: If God gave us a healthy pregnancy, I would give up drinking. Despite the lack of an audible affirmation from the divine, I felt an unwavering commitment to this promise. I'd made my pledge not out of expectation but from a deep-seated desire for change.

A SHIFT IN PERSPECTIVE

As the pregnancy progressed, Jenn's intuition suggested something amiss, and she rushed to the hospital. The congestion of the city meant it would take almost two hours before I could finally join her, an experience that amplified my anxiety and frustration with our living situation. Because this pregnancy was considered high risk because of our previous miscarriages and David's stillbirth, our rocky transition to the East Coast, and our desire to welcome our child into the world in the comfort of the dream home we'd left behind, we decided to leave Virginia and return to Alaska.

The prospect filled me with a secret joy that was overshadowed by the bittersweet realization that Jenn was sacrificing her dream job for our family's well-being. This juxtaposition of the joy of returning home and the sorrow of relinquished dreams mirrored the complexity of our journey. Each step forward was laced with sacrifice, yet it was a path we trod together, bound by love, resilience, and a shared vision for our future.

With our lives taking a new, hopeful direction and the anticipation of welcoming our child, I quickly organized our move back to Alaska. The process was swift, and within a week, everything was arranged. While I was thrilled about returning to our roots, I knew Jenn's emotions were mixed as she grappled with the sorrow of leaving her job behind. Unsure how to ease the transition, I proposed a project to transform our Alaska home into a space that reflected our new beginning. We planned renovations and personal touches, including a custom Pottery Barn couch and setting up our baby's room, a task that temporarily alleviated Jenn's sadness.

Upon our return in March 2011, I immersed myself in the renovations to further personalize our dream home. Being back in Alaska, a place of solitude and refuge, I found some peace. However, the prospect of becoming a stay-at-home dad stirred a familiar whirlwind of anxiety and fear within me. I worried about perpetuating generational cycles of emotional disconnect and doubted my ability to be the father I aspired to be.

These fears dissipated the moment I held my daughter, Kayleigh, for the first time. Her innocence and purity were overwhelming, silencing my insecurities and igniting a profound love I'd never known. The initial days as new parents were a blur of joy and overwhelming responsibility, teaching me the essence of parenthood and the necessity to adapt, learn, and grow alongside my child. Parenting is a journey of constant evolution, and as Kayleigh grew, so did my understanding of my role. I delved into books on parenting, absorbing the consensus that presence is paramount. The commitment to presence became my mantra, and showing up for my daughter was something I committed to wholeheartedly.

Time flew by with Kayleigh in our lives. Celebrating her first birthday in Hawaii, I honored another promise I'd made to God to quit chewing tobacco. This vow, inspired by my daughter and the responsibility of being a role model, proved to be my most challenging battle yet. Still, my desire to be present and healthy for her outweighed the struggle, leading me to finally overcome my addiction.

Our home in Chugiak became more than just a place to live. It was a sanctuary where our daughter's first milestones unfolded. From her initial steps to joyous playtime in the backyard and exhilarating sled rides down the hill, it was our slice of paradise. Amid our bliss, we were overjoyed to learn Jenn was pregnant again. However, this joy was followed by several more miscarriages, each as heart-wrenching as the ones before. Though the losses were somewhat tempered by the presence of our daughter, my struggles with faith and anger persisted, unresolved and complex.

When Jenn announced her ninth pregnancy, my heart soared with hope yet again. Despite my strained relationship with God, I once more found myself on my deck bargaining with Him, clinging to the promise I'd made during Jenn's pregnancy with Kayleigh. I vowed to keep that promise of no alcohol if He gave us another healthy baby. It was a desperate plea, born not from piety, but from the fear of reaching a breaking point. Fortunately, Jenn's pregnancy was remarkably smooth, and we discovered we were expecting a boy whom we decided to name Byron.

With our son's swift arrival in September 2014, my understanding of fatherhood deepened. The responsibility of caring for two young lives was daunting but exhilarating. I had to remind myself that my children were not soldiers; they required a gentleness and patience distinct from the rigid discipline of military life. This realization became a prayer for guidance, a hope to always approach them with the nurturing they deserved, not merely the instruction I thought they needed.

Our family's growth didn't magically resolve my deep-seated fears that I wasn't enough, that I didn't have the emotional capacity to provide the love my kids needed, or that I wouldn't be able to find a pause in heated arguments with Jenn even though I wanted to. But it did shift my perspective. Byron reminded me of the importance of being present and of engaging with my children in ways that fostered their development and happiness. The journey of fatherhood, filled with its unique challenges and joys, became a path to redefining myself — not just as a veteran or a survivor of personal trials, but as a dad committed to the well-being and happiness of the little lives entrusted to me.

Reflecting on this time, it's crucial that I acknowledge the enduring commitment I've maintained to abstaining from alcohol. In the moment of making that vow to God, its full significance was beyond my comprehension. Yet, with the clarity time affords, it's evident that adhering to my promise has been a cornerstone in preserving both my marriage and my life. Marked by moments of profound vulnerability and divine bargaining, the choice to embrace sobriety has been transformative. Although not without its challenges, my decision to stop drinking has unfolded into a pivotal element of my personal growth and stability.

The journey of fatherhood, filled with its unique challenges and joys, became a path to redefining myself – not just as a veteran or a survivor of personal trials, but as a dad committed to the well-being and happiness of the little lives entrusted to me.

My deal with God became more than a plea for a blessing; it evolved into a lifeline that pulled me away from the brink of self-destruction toward a place of strength and renewal. The realization that my commitment was instrumental in preserving the fabric of my family and granted me a second chance at life is a profound acknowledgement of the transformative power of faith, resolve, and the will to forge a better path.

Chapter **6**

LEFT BEHIND

IN THE SUMMER of 2013, I found myself in a rare period of tranquility as I was immersed in the joys and challenges of raising my daughter at our home in Chugiak, Alaska. Despite feeling a renewed sense of purpose through fatherhood, deep down, I was plagued by feelings of inadequacy. My internal dialogue was incessant, oscillating between self-assurance in my role as a father and the fear of ultimately failing my family.

At the same time, it became evident that our marriage was struggling, and Jenn was grappling with her own profound issues as she balanced her health, work, and role as a mother. My own battles with anger, frustration, and deep-seated hurt clouded my ability to see and understand her struggles. Our attempts to communicate often degenerated into arguments, exacerbating my self-doubt and reinforcing to Jenn an image of indifference that couldn't be further from the truth. I was trapped in a cycle of internalizing my problems, a method of coping I mistakenly expected Jenn to adopt as well. It was during this time that

Jenn and I began to contemplate selling our dream home to move closer to her family in Anchorage.

The decision to sell our home, our sanctuary, was fraught with mixed emotions. The thought of leaving stirred my fears of loss and regret, revealing a hesitancy I struggled to communicate to Jenn. I believed moving was what she desired and hoped it would bring her solace, unaware that she harbored similar reservations. However, the prospect of moving closer to Jenn's family seemed to lift a weight off her shoulders, and I resolved to support whatever decision was necessary for our well-being, even if it meant parting with the home that embodied our dreams.

As we discussed the potential for another new beginning, it became clear that both of us were navigating our pain in isolation, neither fully honest about the extent of our emotional wounds. The eventual decision to sell our home was a choice born not out of defeat but out of a mutual recognition of our need for healing and support. We believed this move would be a step toward mending our relationship and rebuilding our lives with the well-being of our family at the forefront.

MAKING THE BEST OF THE CIRCUMSTANCES

Navigating the bittersweet process of selling our cherished home and seeking a new beginning closer to family was more challenging than we anticipated. The limited and costly housing market starkly contrasted with the haven we were leaving behind, making each property we viewed seem lacking. Once again, I reverted to my usual coping mechanisms and buried my emotions in the logistics of the move until they surfaced in moments of overwhelming stress. Throughout this transition, our dogs, Apollo and Sapphire, remained my anchors. Apollo, specifically, seemed to possess an innate understanding of my struggles and provided comfort without judgment.

Eventually, we found a house within walking distance of Jenn's parents, but I had some concerns about what I saw as I walked through the home. During the inspection, it was clear the house had been jacked up and leveled out because of sinking due to improper foundation work, a fixable, yet expensive, issue. This discovery led us to withdraw our offer, plunging us back into an uncertain search. Settling on a house still under construction, we faced compromises, particularly in construction quality, which was notably inferior to what we were accustomed to. My background in construction allowed me to mitigate some concerns, but the experience was fraught with frustration and disappointment.

Our final night in our dream home culminated in the worst argument Jenn and I'd ever had. The empty house echoed with our raised voices, a painful cacophony of years of pent-up anger and hurt. Regret for the words I unleashed that night still lingers, a reminder of a moment when I failed to be the partner Jenn deserved.

Transitioning to temporary quarters on Elmendorf Air Force Base while our new home was being built brought an unexpected peace. I found solace in the familiarity and security of the base, enjoying restful nights for the first time in a long while. However, we weren't allowed to keep the dogs with us during our stay, and Apollo's absence underscored his significant role in my well-being. Not only did I feel disconnected without Apollo and Sapphire, but our daughter, Kayleigh, missed her protective companions and playmates.

As we put the finishing touches on our new home, the upcoming landscaping project became a surprising battleground. Our detailed plans, including tree removal for safety reasons recommended by an arborist, were met with unexpected resistance from the HOA, sparking a confrontation with the HOA's vice president, a fellow soldier, that felt like an all too familiar reminder of past conflicts. This incident stirred the deep-seated anger I continued to wrestle with, and much like my argument with Jenn the night before we moved, I chose to bury my anger and forge ahead. Recognizing the futility of direct confrontation with the HOA, I opted to hire a lawyer. The swift resolution that followed the lawyer's intervention brought the approval we needed but no satisfaction.

With the HOA's approval finally secured and our beloved dogs back with us in our new home, life began to feel like it was on an upward trajectory. Even though my anger was a constant companion, the commencement of the yard work brought a tangible sense of progress and fulfillment. Those long days spent reshaping our outdoor space, with Kayleigh eagerly participating in everything from steering a Bobcat to laying conduit for lighting, were moments of pure connection.

By summer's end, our yard was transformed. What had been a patch of dirt was now lush with dark green Kentucky bluegrass, the trees artfully lit by landscape lighting, creating a serene oasis that mirrored our vision for the space. This transformation symbolized more than just a successful landscaping project; it represented healing and the creation of a new sanctuary for my family within the confines of what our community allowed.

THE CHASM BETWEEN US

During this period of renewal and hard work, Jenn was pregnant with Byron, adding layers of anticipation and joy to our daily lives. And emboldened by the progress we'd made on our home, I decided to further my education in construction and construction management. Despite the chaos of preparing to welcome another family member, I felt a cautious optimism that perhaps we were indeed moving into a chapter where the past's shadows might finally be outpaced by the promise of tomorrow.

However, amid these hopeful developments, I began experiencing intense, unexplained bouts of pain. These episodes, sharp and severe, were fleeting yet becoming more frequent. Reluctant to detract from the positive momentum we were building, I chose silence. Burying these alarming symptoms, as I had so many worries before, I continued to struggle between seeking genuine happiness and the instinct to suppress vulnerability.

A busy fall culminated with Byron's birth and a fleeting honeymoon phase in the ongoing challenges and unspoken struggles within our marriage. Despite the external appearance of unity and the fresh start we'd hoped this new home would bring us, we were still silently navigating our own tumultuous paths.

Jenn sought solace in faith, finding comfort in the community and spiritual guidance of a church. This endeavor was largely a solitary journey for her as my response to our situation was not to seek peace through faith but to retreat further into my anger. It was a choice that isolated me from her efforts to find a sanctuary for herself and our children. Though I occasionally accompanied Jenn to church, knowing it meant a lot to her, my presence there was not as a partner in faith but as a silent challenger to God. My prayers were replaced with a tirade of questions and accusations, leaving me drained and even more distant from the experience Jenn was embracing. This disparity made my sporadic attempts to join her in church not a bridge over our divide but a reminder of the chasm between us.

I now realize that every visit to the church lightened Jenn's burden slightly, offering her a respite I struggled to understand or support fully at the time. My failure to openly support my wife or to share my inner turmoil only deepened the wounds in our marriage. While we both made efforts to navigate the complexities of our relationship and to heal the growing rifts, my approach — living in a state of anger and withdrawal — had a profound impact on Jenn. The choices I made and the way I coped with our circumstances not only hindered my own healing but also inflicted unseen scars on my wife, scars that I was too wrapped up in my own pain to recognize.

A SENSE OF BETRAYAL

Our first Christmas with Byron brought a sense of completeness to our family, but the post-Christmas calm was abruptly shattered when Apollo, usually a source of

The choices I made and the way I coped with our circumstances not only hindered my own healing but also inflicted unseen scars on my wife, scars that I was too wrapped up in my own pain to recognize.

unwavering loyalty and comfort, acted out in a moment of jealousy and bit Kayleigh half an inch below her left eye. The aftermath was chaos. Jenn was in a panic at the sight of Kayleigh's injury. I immediately reverted to my military training and took calm and decisive action, yet inside, my heart was racing, my anger boiling over the top. Although the bite was severe enough that I was afraid Kayleigh would have permanent damage, I maintained a cool demeanor with the help of my dad and mom, who had been visiting for Christmas.

The hospital visit underscored the gravity of the situation. As doctors prepared Kayleigh for surgery to minimize scarring from the bite, Jenn and I found ourselves united in silence, a pattern all too familiar in our relationship. This incident, a harsh pivot from our holiday happiness, was a reminder of the unpredictability of life and how quickly joy can turn to despair.

Kayleigh's resilience in the face of trauma was nothing short of miraculous. Her surgery was executed by one of Alaska's best plastic surgeons, and we returned home hopeful but burdened. The moment we stepped through our door, Kayleigh's display of forgiveness toward Apollo was a profound lesson in love and grace, something I felt I knew nothing about. Despite her innocence and readiness to forgive, the safety of my children took precedence. Apollo was muzzled and underwent exhaustive veterinary consultations to seek any underlying cause for his behavior.

Unfortunately, the conclusion was heartbreakingly clear: Apollo had become possessive over me and my time and could no longer be trusted around children. Our vet and trainer both suggested rehoming Apollo to a child-free environment, but the thought of separating him from his littermate, Sapphire, and our family was agonizing. The decision to rehome them together, while logical, amplified my sense of loss. This was not merely about finding them a new home; it was about severing a bond that had been a source of comfort and strength for me as I struggled to transition into my role outside of the military.

The process of rehoming Apollo and Sapphire became an insurmountable task. The drive to deliver the dogs to our friend's kennel was laden with grief and the sense that I'd betrayed my companions. Knowing I would never see them again, the military adage "never leave a fallen comrade behind" haunted me, highlighting the gravity of my perceived failure to both of my loyal friends. Struggling to reconcile my beliefs about loyalty and protection and grappling with the harsh reality of the decisions we are sometimes forced to make even when they tear at the very fabric of our hearts, I found myself once again forgetting to check in with Jenn about her daily experiences or her well-being.

THE CHAOS BEHIND THE FACADE

When Jenn announced she was being transferred to Indianapolis, Indiana, I was momentarily speechless — a rare occurrence for someone who is never at a loss for words. Her revelation was a statement, not a request, that left me reeling. My entire adult life had been a journey away from Indiana and toward the mountains I'd dreamed of since I was nineteen. This government-paid move meant that our recently built home would have to be sold, and we would once again need to uproot our lives. The prospect of moving, although outwardly met with a smile and feigned enthusiasm, unleashed a storm of dread and anger at the thought of returning to the very place I'd sought to escape from.

This turn of events forced me to confront the reality of how disconnected I'd become from Jenn. The move to Indiana was another wake-up call to reengage with my partner, to bridge the gaps that had formed between us, and to face whatever lay ahead in this next chapter of our lives.

Moving day approached at a frantic pace, and I found myself juggling the logistic challenges of our relocation with my duties as a father. I did my best to paint a picture of excitement about the move and ensure our children felt loved and secure, especially Kayleigh, whose young world was about to be upended. It was during this chaos that I accidentally left our bedroom door open as I was preparing my firearms for transport. Exploring the space in his walker, Byron ventured out of the room and headed straight for the stairs. Despite my desperate attempts to reach him in time, I watched in horror as he tumbled down to the main floor. Racing after Byron, I was consumed by a singular focus to minimize his injuries. But the damage was done.

As the ambulance rushed us to the hospital, the quiet beeps of the heart monitor and the shallowness of his breaths haunted me with the possibility of losing him. Watching the hospital's trauma response team leap into action to care for Byron, I was confronted with the weight of my responsibilities and my deep-seated belief that I should bear the burden of any misfortune that befell our family. Miraculously, after thorough examinations at the hospital, Byron was declared unscathed by the fall. This incident caused me to reckon with my own limitations and the understanding that some outcomes are beyond my control, no matter how fiercely I wished otherwise.

In the days that followed, our household rebounded swiftly, regaining a semblance of normalcy. However, behind my mask of strength and stability, I struggled to process my emotions. More than ever, I felt the void created by Apollo's absence in my life, and I realized his companionship had been a cornerstone of my stability, akin to that of a service dog. As I worked to process Byron's fall, my inability to forgive myself and my feelings of failure remained acute but largely unnoticed by those around me, amplifying my sense of isolation.

I knew our move from Alaska to Indiana represented more than just a change in location; it was a step into an uncertain future. Settling into our temporary apartment in Carmel, Indiana, and beginning the house-hunting process yet again, I found myself engulfed in loss and guilt. The absence of our dogs was a constant reminder of my failure, not just to them but to my family. My inability to protect Byron from harm and the feeling that I was letting Kayleigh down compounded into a maelstrom of anger and frustration that created a pervasive fog, a darkness that obscured my ability to engage with the present and clouded my judgment and perspective.

Chapter 7

BUYING A LEMON

HOUSE HUNTING, in theory, should have been an exciting endeavor, especially with Indiana's reasonable housing market and our healthy budget. Our main criteria — an in-ground pool — narrowed our options, but despite viewing numerous properties, we struggled to find one that truly felt like the right fit. This challenge was compounded by our cramped living situation in a small, two-bedroom apartment, which made the urgency to find and secure a suitable home feel even more pressing.

It was with this sense of urgency that we revisited a house we'd previously dismissed. However, this time, with a deliberate effort to view it with fresh eyes, I found myself drawn to the impressively large in-ground pool in the backyard, complete with a water slide. The potential cost and value of such an amenity made me reconsider other aspects of the house I'd initially labeled as inadequate. Neither Jenn nor I was particularly thrilled about the house, yet the practical benefits it offered — being well under our budget, featuring the desired pool, and located in an area known for its excellent schools — weighed heavily on our decision-making. After spending a considerable amount of time reassessing the property, the fear of remaining without a permanent home made us decide that this house, despite our reservations, might be the sensible choice.

As we started the purchasing process, I engaged a home inspector for a thorough examination of both the house and the pool. During the inspection, I followed the inspector closely, noticing far more issues than I had during our initial visit. A particular concern arose in the basement while inspecting the furnace and water heater. Spotting some droppings, I questioned whether they were signs of mice. The inspector assured me it was likely insulation debris and not something to fret over. Never having mice in our homes before, combined with the inspector's reassurance, led me to accept his explanation without further suspicion.

The rest of the inspection revealed mostly superficial and cosmetic issues, and we requested the seller address a few key concerns, such as installing a new sump pump to prevent potential basement flooding. Though the inspection wasn't alarming, the purchase process became unexpectedly challenging because of a less-than-stellar realtor and equally difficult sellers. Our frustration peaked when, just twenty-four hours before closing, we found the house in a deplorable state, with trash scattered everywhere and holes in the walls. It felt as though we were reliving our previous experience moving to Virginia and that our significant investment mattered little to everyone involved in the sale.

Confronted with this disrespect, I informed our realtor in no uncertain terms that unless the house was cleaned to our satisfaction before the final signing, we would with-draw from the purchase, forfeit our earnest money, and sever our relationship with her. My ultimatum was deliv-ered without warning to Jenn, leaving her momentarily unsure of how to react. As we left the property, I shared my sentiments with Jenn and remained resolute in my stance that our investment deserved respect. My refusal to engage further until assurances of the house's cleanliness were met was a stand against the lack of professionalism and a stand for the respect and decency our family's com-mitment warranted.

The next morning, our realtor assured me via text that the house had been cleaned and all unwanted items removed. Although the cleanliness wasn't quite to our standards, we proceeded with the closing. However, un-beknownst to us, closing on a house in Indiana involves both the buyers and sellers, and as we moved into the clos-ing room, we were greeted by the sellers and their realtor. Not being informed of this felt like an ambush that cast a shadow over what should have been a joyful occasion.

Like all challenges in our relationship, Jenn and I bore the brunt of this experience silently, each of us process-ing the situation in our own way. I couldn't help but feel partly responsible for the negative turn the transaction had taken. Though I believed my actions were justified, the cumulative effect of these adversities began to erode the optimism we had for a fresh start in our new, albeit "used," home. The prospect of beginning anew, once a bea-con of hope, seemed to diminish with each hurdle we en-countered, leaving us to ponder the path forward against a backdrop of continued uncertainty.

BLOW AFTER BLOW

Shortly after finalizing the purchase of our home in June 2015, our household goods from Alaska arrived, heralding a new wave of chaos. Among other mishaps, the movers, seemingly indifferent to the care of our belongings, accidentally slashed several couch cushions with a razor blade. The disarray of our possessions mirrored my own internal disintegration, the destruction emblematic of the broader upheaval we'd experienced since leaving Alaska.

In the midst of unpacking and setting up our new home, we rushed to prepare for Kayleigh's fourth birthday. We planned a pool party to celebrate, inviting family from across Indiana. This reunion with loved ones I hadn't seen in years and the joy of introducing them to my daughter and son momentarily lifted the cloud of gloom. The warmth and love of family underscored the potential for happiness in our new setting, offering a glimmer of why life in Indiana might not be as bleak as I'd feared.

However, just days after the birthday celebrations, I was plunged back into a state of chaos and frustration. Hearing Jenn scream while breastfeeding our son sent me running upstairs, only to be met by a mouse scurrying directly toward me. My reaction, a startled scream, turned into a moment of levity as Jenn and Kayleigh laughed. The chase that ensued ended with the mouse darting under the stove, leading us to discover a hole heading into the basement.

This discovery prompted a thorough inspection of the mechanical room, where I had previously questioned the home inspector about what I suspected were mouse droppings. His reassurance now rang hollow as the evidence of our rodent issue became undeniable. Further investigation revealed significant holes in the house's structure because of unaddressed gaps from a furnace installation done by the previous owners. The realization that we were dealing not just with a solitary mouse, but a potentially larger infestation was a hard pill to swallow. This revelation was yet another blow, a stark reminder of the unforeseen challenges that lay hidden beneath the surface of our new beginning.

In preparation for the arrival of Jenn's parents for a visit, I decided to hire an exterminator to address the issue of the mice while I patched up the visible holes, tackling the problem with the level of seriousness it needed and deserved. The joy of showcasing our new pool and sharing my home state with them was a welcome distraction; however, a few days into their stay, I noticed a worrying wet spot on the ceiling beneath the main upstairs bathroom. Initially, the spot seemed minor, but the dampness grew over time, indicating a hidden leak. Midway through her parents' visit, I couldn't ignore the growing wet spot any longer. Concerned about potential black mold, I cut into the ceiling and was relieved to find the damage was localized and the joists in good condition, albeit stained. My relief was short-lived as further investigation in the upstairs bathroom unveiled a distressing sight. Beneath the laminate flooring and behind the walls, black mold was rampant, necessitating a complete gutting of the bathroom down to the studs for a thorough remediation.

Standing amid the unfolding disaster, I grappled with feelings of failure. My professional background in housing and construction made this oversight feel even more personal. While it was easiest to direct my frustration at the previous owners, the realtor, the home inspector, and even fate itself, deep down, I knew this was just the tip of the iceberg. This series of household calamities not only highlighted the unforeseen challenges of homeownership but also tested my resilience, forcing me to confront the realities of our new home head-on.

In the wake of already overwhelming issues, our situation further deteriorated a few months later. To accommodate the renovations initiated by contractors I'd hired, we moved most of our belongings to the basement, transforming it into a temporary storage area. One morning, as I was about to prepare breakfast for Kayleigh and Byron, I realized the necessary dishes were in the basement. Descending the stairs, I was met with water seeping across the floor and our possessions adrift in the flood. The sump pump, which the previous owners claimed to have replaced — as evidenced by a receipt — had failed, leading to a flooded basement. Upon inspecting this "new" sump pump, we saw that the manufacturing date was listed as 2003, which meant the previous owners had lied.

The discovery pushed me to a new low, the depth of which I had never experienced. Overwhelmed by anger and frustration, these emotions fueled my initial response to the crisis. Despite Jenn's attempts to communicate with me throughout the ordeal, my overwhelming anger formed an impenetrable barrier between us. Jenn was incredibly supportive, a true pillar of strength during those trying times, but the flood's aftermath demanded nearly a full day's effort to mitigate. We were forced to remove and discard the newly laid carpet, cut away the soaked drywall and baseboards, and find a way to salvage and dry out our waterlogged belongings.

This incident felt like a symbolic loss of everything we had worked so hard to build. With each new problem that arose with the house, my sense of inadequacy and worthlessness deepened. At the same time, despite my genuine efforts to overcome my anger and frustration and communicate my needs, I was acutely aware of how my coping mechanisms for managing emotions, hardships, and challenges were causing pain to those I loved most. Although I strove to embody the fresh start I so deeply desired for my wife and children, I felt as though we were perpetually sinking under the weight of continuous and relentless challenges.

THE MOMENT OF RECKONING

To the world around me, my struggles were visibly manifesting. My weight gain and the change in my demeanor painted a starkly different picture from the person I once was. When I spoke of my past as a scout sniper, I could sense the disbelief in people's gazes, a silent questioning of my truth, which only deepened my sense of disconnect between the man I aspired to be and the person I'd become.

In the fall of 2015, Dustin, a friend from my scout sniper platoon, visited me in Indiana. Although he was someone with whom I'd once shared everything, I kept silent about the storm brewing within me, my discovery of Jenn's search for a local divorce lawyer, and the tumultuous feelings eating away at my mental and physical health that made me believe I was digging my own grave. His visit was

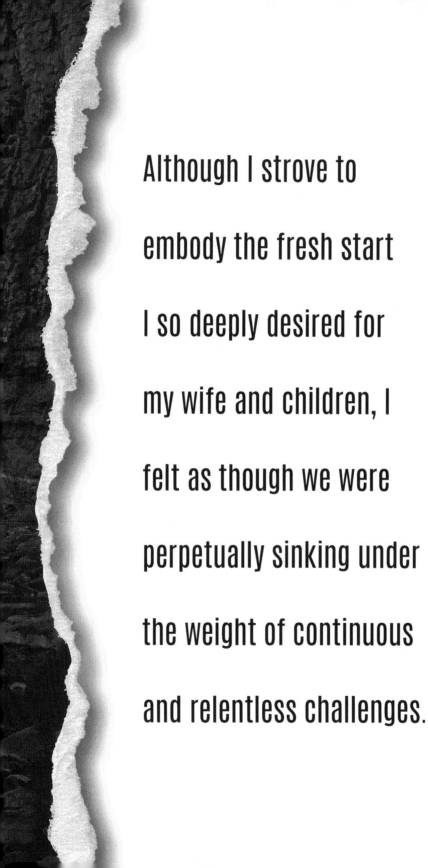

Although I strove to

embody the fresh start

I so deeply desired for

my wife and children, I

felt as though we were

perpetually sinking under

the weight of continuous

and relentless challenges.

a temporary escape, and despite the promise I'd made to God to abstain from drinking, I rationalized breaking that vow, telling myself that just one beer would be harmless. One beer blurred into many, reviving my "Frank the Tank" persona for a night of forgetfulness and abandon.

The subsequent sickness lasted for days and was a painful reminder of my broken promise, sinking me further into despair. I couldn't see past the multitude of ways I felt I'd let my family down. My nightmares wouldn't let up. My health was deteriorating. My joy and pride in being a husband and father were overshadowed by a pervasive sense of inadequacy, anger, and frustration. The knowledge that Jenn was contemplating divorce only compounded these feelings, leading me to a point of utter hopelessness.

I couldn't envision a way forward where my efforts would amount to anything meaningful. In this darkened state of mind, the thought of ending my life emerged as a viable escape from the unending cycle of failure. I'd reached my breaking point, believing that my absence might be a relief to those I loved most, blinded to the devastation such an act would inflict.

Resolute in my decision, I sat calmly at the table I'd so proudly built months earlier, contemplating the end. However, despite my attempts to pull the trigger, the sight of the clock shook me from my daze and reminded me of my responsibility to pick up my children from daycare. It was this obligation, this promise to them, that halted my actions. I couldn't fail at this one final thing. Perhaps, subconsciously, I was seeking a reason, any reason, not to follow through with my despairing thoughts. Putting away my weapon, picking up my kids, and most importantly, calling my best friend Brent to ask for help, I cracked open the door to discover the support I needed.

I felt lighter.

A few weeks later, I found myself standing at the bottom of the staircase, looking up at Jenn and opening up in a way I'd never done before. I don't remember my exact words, but I know it was a confession, an acknowledgement of my inner turmoil. I said something like, "Maybe God had us buy this house because the way it looks on the outside mirrors how I feel and look on the inside. And maybe as I fix this house up, I'll fix myself in the process." Admitting the chaos within me was the first step toward vulnerability with my wife. Her response was a simple smile and a reassuring hug, and although she may not have grasped the full weight of my admission, it didn't matter to me because I'd finally put it out there.

This moment sparked a dual path of reconstruction of our home and of my psyche. Following through on my commitment to Brent, I applied to the No Barriers program, pouring my truth into the application, omitting only the darkest of my recent thoughts. My acceptance into the program coincided with the day of my grandmother's burial and felt like an opportunity for redemption.

Preparing for the No Barriers program, coupled with my growing attendance at church, began to erode the layers of anger and resentment encasing me. Each sermon, each quiet moment spent in reflection, peeled away the bitterness — though my contention with God remained a fierce dialogue of unanswered questions. At the same time, the renovation of our home became my physical and metaphorical rebuilding project.

Over the course of seven years, each repair, each improvement, was a step toward not just a house restored but a man reformed. The process was my meditation, my penance, and my therapy, culminating in a home that, while outwardly beautiful and perfect, held too many ghosts of my past selves. In 2022, with the house and, to a significant extent, myself reconstructed, the decision to sell and move on was both a practical choice influenced by the market and a deeply personal need to leave behind the site of my lowest point. The sale of the house, swift and profitable, was not just a financial win. It was a milestone marking how far I'd journeyed from the brink of despair to a place of strength and resilience. Closing this chapter was a celebration of survival and growth — a testament to the fact that while we may be handed challenges, those challenges forge our strength and character. To me, it felt like a declaration that the past, no matter how painful, could be the foundation for a brighter, hopeful future.

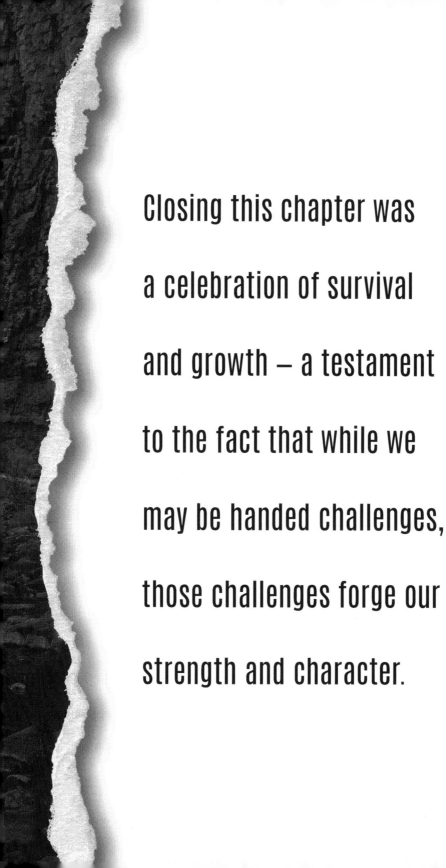

Closing this chapter was

a celebration of survival

and growth – a testament

to the fact that while we

may be handed challenges,

those challenges forge our

strength and character.

Chapter 8

REFUGE ON THE RIVER

OVER THE NEXT several months, Jenn and I began to rediscover some closeness. It wasn't perfect, but our communication evolved from ignoring or yelling at each other to sitting and talking. I did my best to show Jenn the changes I was striving to make by applying to veterans' programs and regularly attending church. I even tried to get to know our senior pastor, whose sermons seemed to speak directly to me. Although I hadn't lost any weight, I began focusing on my health and experienced a noticeable difference in how I felt. I also began making progress on projects around the house. I still struggled with stress management, often internalizing it until I couldn't hold it in any longer or mishandling situations from the start, and I spent too much time trying to control the outcomes of our life scenarios, but I was trying.

As June 2016 approached, we both felt optimistic about the upcoming opportunity to connect with fellow veterans in No Barriers USA's Warriors program, which aimed to help participants realize their best selves. Their motto,

"What's within you is stronger than what's in your way," resonated with me and gave me hope that I possessed the strength to overcome my challenges.

My first expedition with No Barriers was supposed to be in the Wind River Range of Wyoming, a place I'd climbed in my early twenties. Unfortunately, just weeks before departure, our permit was revoked due to high avalanche risks from that year's heavy snowpack. While most organizations might have canceled the trip, No Barriers saw it as an opportunity to exemplify their philosophy of overcoming obstacles, and they quickly pivoted and planned a new seven-day trek through the Gila National Forest along the West Fork Gila River.

When I learned we'd be heading to the desert instead of the mountains, my gut reaction was a firm no. My last desert experience during my deployment was far from positive, and I was reluctant to return. However, sharing my thoughts with Jenn led to a grim reality check. Her words were clear and tinged with finality: "Eric, if you don't go, we might end up divorced. I don't want that, but I can't continue in our current life. It's your choice, but if you decide not to go, it could mean the end of us." The gravity of her statement and my deep love for her and our children spurred me into action. Despite my reservations, I packed my bags and committed to doing whatever it took to mend our fraying ties.

The day I departed for the Gila National Forest was the first time I'd been away from my children since their births. As a stay-at-home dad, I was a constant presence, and the thought of not being there to protect them filled me with anxiety. I also feared how my recurring nightmares would play out in the close quarters of a tent I'd have to share with others, and the possibility of embarrassing myself in front of my tentmates weighed heavily on me. Nonetheless, Jenn, Kayleigh, and Byron's support as they saw me off at the airport bolstered my spirits. Jenn's look of love, respect, and appreciation was a reminder of why I was undertaking this journey.

THE CANYON OF HOPE

As I walked through the airport security gate, my mind was dominated by gratitude for a family who loved me unconditionally and recognition that this trip was not just another departure; it was the beginning of a transformative journey. I was starting from a place lower than rock bottom, having just begun to climb out of the deep hole I'd dug for myself. This trip was about more than just survival; it was about accepting the necessity of being reforged, confronting the fears that might cause me to lose parts of myself in the process. I understood that this journey wouldn't solve everything but instead represented a critical pivot toward a new way of living. It was going to be a marathon filled with hard truths I'd need to confront. This was the first step in a long process of change, a commitment to move forward differently and more consciously.

I flew from Indianapolis to El Paso, Texas, where the group — twelve veterans and four staff members — would gather before our journey. We crammed our gear into one of two big, white passenger vans and climbed into the other before setting off for Silver City, New Mexico. That

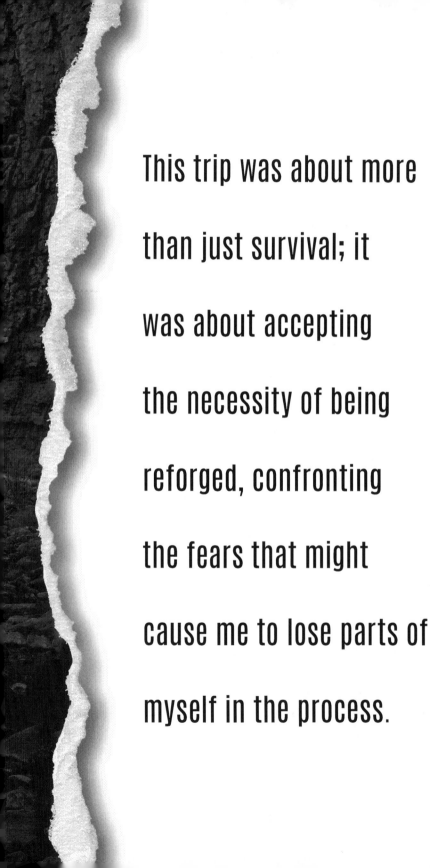

This trip was about more than just survival; it was about accepting the necessity of being reforged, confronting the fears that might cause me to lose parts of myself in the process.

evening was spent on quiet introductions and preparations as we ate dinner together, completed gear checks, and set expectations for the days ahead. Surrounded by the easy camaraderie of others, I found myself unusually reserved. To mask my fears about being away from my children and my precarious emotional state, I mimicked the happiness around me, a skill well-honed from years of practice.

Jenn, thoughtful as ever, had given me pages of a devotional she'd torn from her copy of *Jesus Calling* by Sarah Young, each page bearing a note encouraging me to start my day reflecting on what God might be trying to communicate. However, instead of starting my day with the devotional as intended, I decided to read them at the end of each day, hoping to prove to myself that these messages had no real influence over my day-to-day experiences. That night, overwhelmed and sharing a room with a stranger, I forgot to read the first page entirely.

The next morning, I woke up feeling terribly unwell, another reminder of how little control I had over anything at that moment. A full-on flare-up of my Fibromyalgia forced me to immediately start a prednisone pack, but unfortunately, the long ride to the trailhead worsened my condition, and I found myself rushing to an outhouse to vomit within minutes of our arrival. A bit of water and fresh air gradually eased my nausea, and as we descended into a lush canyon, I was struck by the serene beauty of our surroundings. It was a moment of unexpected peace, a glimpse of the healing power of nature I'd almost forgotten.

Our initial trek led us through a valley marked by the aftermath of severe fires and flooding. The sparse, knee-high grasses and charred alligator juniper trees, still clinging to life despite their scorched bark, resonated deeply with me. Their damage mirrored the turmoil within me, and each step revealed a reflection of my struggles for me to capture through the lens of my camera. This profound connection made the journey feel significant right from the start.

That first day, we covered just a few miles to focus on establishing our camp routines. Learning how to set up tents, cook together, and distribute responsibilities was crucial for the cohesion of our group. Our campsite, nestled in a clearing amid the resilient alligator juniper trees, became a tranquil home for the night. As darkness enveloped us, the sky revealed a breathtaking tapestry of stars, prompting me to stay up late to photograph the new world above me. When I finally returned to my tent, I read the first of Jenn's *Jesus Calling* messages. It urged trust over fear and strength over struggle, reminding me that my perceived weaknesses were drawing me closer to a greater intimacy with life's deeper forces. The message resonated with my surroundings and my journey, reinforcing that I wasn't alone. It read:

> "*TRUST ME and don't be afraid, for I am your Strength and Song.* Do not let fear dissipate your energy. Instead, invest your energy in trusting Me and singing My Song. The battle for control of your mind is fierce, and years of worry have made you vulnerable to the enemy. Therefore, you need to be vigilant in guarding your thoughts. Do not despise this weakness in yourself, since I am using it to draw you closer to Me. Your constant need

for Me creates an intimacy that is well worth all the effort. You are not alone in this struggle for your mind. My Spirit living within you is ever ready to help in this striving. Ask Him to *control your mind*; He will bless you with *Life and Peace*."[1]

The night swiftly turned to morning as we woke to prepare for the day's trek. Our morning routine was a well-orchestrated dance of making breakfast, packing tents, and gearing up that took roughly two hours before we were back on the trail. Descending into a deep canyon, the scene before me was nothing short of mesmerizing, and after a few miles of hiking, we reached the West Fork Gila River, another stunning spectacle of nature's beauty.

Standing in the shadows of the canyon, I was struck by the persistent light at the end of the gorge. Again, I saw my journey reflected in my surroundings, and the canyon seemed to say that no matter the darkness surrounding me, there was always light ahead. This imagery of light prevailing over shadows influenced me deeply and became the dominant theme of my expedition. I spent considerable time capturing this metaphor through my camera lens, seeking to find that one perfect shot to hang in my office as a reminder of hope during dark times. That one shot, *Canyon of Hope*, has gone on to win awards and hangs proudly in the heart of my home. It also became the cover of this book.

1 Young, Sarah. 2011. *Jesus Calling: Enjoying Peace in His Presence (A 365-Day Devotional)*. Nashville, Tennessee: Thomas Nelson.

SEEING THE GARDEN BEYOND THE THORNS

The days passed quickly and were filled with profound conversations around the campfire with fellow veterans. During one of these discussions, an expedition leader shared an insight that stuck with me. He said that between every stimulus and response lies a space, and our power lies in how we use that space to shape our reactions. This concept was revelatory. It was the first time I'd considered creating space to allow for more thoughtful responses rather than the instantaneous reactions trained into me by the military.

At our last campsite of the trip, the atmosphere was a mix of relaxation and subtle anxiety. The campsite itself offered both delightful and unnerving experiences. One of the highlights was a thermal pool fed by the river, providing a perfect respite for our tired muscles after a week of trekking with heavy packs. However, the presence of numerous snakes around the campsite added an element of fear to our serene surroundings. Given the deep spiritual reflections I'd experienced throughout the trip, encountering these snakes felt symbolic of the internal battles I was facing.

As the evening unfolded, it became a time for both celebration of our journey and contemplation of the future. The mood was tinged with a sense of trepidation about returning to our usual lives, making the moments around the campfire particularly poignant. That night, surrounded by my teammates, I struggled to hold back tears as I read another torn piece of Jenn's *Jesus Calling* devotional. It said:

"*I HAVE LOVED YOU with an everlasting Love.* Before time began, I knew you. For years you swam around in a sea of meaninglessness, searching for Love, hoping for hope. All that time I was pursuing you, aching to embrace you in My compassionate arms. When time was right, I revealed Myself to you. I lifted you out of that sea of despair and set you down on a firm foundation. Sometimes you felt naked—exposed to the revealing Light of My Presence. I wrapped an ermine robe around you: *My robe of righteousness.* I sang you a Love song, whose beginning and end are veiled in eternity. I infused meaning into your mind and harmony into your heart. Join Me in singing My song. Together we will draw others out of darkness into *My marvelous Light.*"[2]

I allowed myself to sit in my emotions for a moment, and before long, my tent mates and I were in our tent laughing our asses off. Our jokes, too inappropriate to recount here, sparked the kind of laughter that's deep and true, the kind that stitches people together. It was a laughter I hadn't enjoyed in years, and it replenished something deep inside me. Settling into my sleeping bag, the joy of the evening mingled with the anxiety of returning to everyday life.

These conflicting feelings brewed a storm within me, and soon, the very dream I feared most began to unfold.

---

2 Young, Sarah. 2011. *Jesus Calling: Enjoying Peace in His Presence (A 365-Day Devotional).* Nashville, Tennessee: Thomas Nelson.

I was back with my family at the Santa Monica Miramar, a scene that shifted rapidly from a peaceful moment to an unfolding nightmare at the corner of Wilshire and Ocean. But this time, I felt an intense presence, and, in desperation, I threw up my hands and cried out to God. I said, "I can't do this alone anymore. I need your help."

My dream shifted, and the nightmare dissipated into the purest white I'd ever seen, brilliant but gentle on the eyes. As I steadied my breath, a figure approached. Not just any figure but one who radiated a sense of love that matched my visions of who Jesus might be. As He drew near, my years of pent-up anger burst forth. There were no greetings or grateful words; instead, I unleashed a decade's worth of pain and bitterness directly at Him. From personal grievances to broader existential laments about society, I railed against Him with every accusation I could muster. Yet, through my fury, His response was simple and filled with unconditional love.

"Eric, I've been with you the whole time," He said calmly, absorbing my rage without flinching. "The anger you've nurtured has blinded you, Eric. You haven't been able to see past it to see Me or the path I laid out for you."

This confrontation, intense and raw, brought me clarity and revealed the deep-seated barriers that had isolated me from divine presence and peace.

Then, Jesus pointed out the stark contrast between how I viewed myself and how He and His Father saw me. "You are shrouded in shame, but it's not how we see you," He expressed patiently.

He invited me to follow Him, and, after a sudden change in scenery, we found ourselves in a vast, breathtaking garden brimming with all my favorite trees and flowers: dogwoods, magnolia trees, roses, tulips, daisies, fireweed, along with fruiting apple and cherry trees. It was unlike anything I'd ever seen.

"This garden," Jesus explained as we wandered, "represents your potential, your soul. But you can't see it because your vision is clouded by anger, by the bad. The challenges you've faced? They're meant to draw you closer to us, to forge your character, and align you closer to your destiny." He was candid about the journey ahead and said, "Building this garden won't be easy. It will hurt. And often, you won't see the immediate impact of your efforts. Remember this garden, Eric, when you feel lost."

Then, as if to illustrate a point, the scene shifted dramatically to an intimidating and nearly impassable thicket of briars and thorns. "This thicket," He continued, "is what your anger has created around you. Clearing this and starting anew will be tough but necessary. As you work through this, look to your left, and you'll find me there, walking beside you. You are never alone."

As quickly as He had appeared, Jesus was gone, and I awoke to a new morning filled with an unfamiliar sense of hope and joy for the first time in years. His words lingered, a guide for the profound personal work ahead.

EMBRACING THE JOURNEY

We efficiently broke up camp and were on the trail in no time. A few hours into our trek, during a water break, our expedition leaders suggested we take some time alone to reflect on the past week, the lessons learned, the personal growth experienced, and the new tools we'd each gathered. I welcomed the idea of solitary contemplation, especially after the intense revelations of the previous night's dream.

Alone with my thoughts, I navigated the path, each step a chance to decompress and consider the transformative experiences of the journey. About forty-five minutes into this solitary walk, I encountered our trip's photographer. His career, capturing life through lenses in remote and sometimes volatile environments, was, at one time, a dream of mine, and I loved hearing his stories. As we walked, our conversation drifted to the logistics of working in less-secure areas. I was particularly interested in how he managed safety concerns, prompting him to share insights about working with local fixers and coordinating with local authorities to ensure security. However, his final comment resonated most profoundly with me. He said, "In the end, Eric, you just have to have faith in the goodness of the human spirit."

This simple advice echoed the lessons of trust and resilience I was learning to embrace, reminding me that beyond all strategies and precautions, it's the fundamental belief in human kindness that often carries us through. Left alone with the photographer's words echoing in my mind, I found myself deep in thought. The idea that one must simply have faith in the goodness of the human spirit made me realize my fundamental issue: I suffered from a profound lack of faith.

Reflecting on my experiences, I remembered a conversation from years ago when someone asked me to describe what it was like to be in war. I likened it to an episode from Seinfeld involving "Bubble Boy," drawing a parallel to how individuals are encased in a metaphorical bubble of innocence that life inevitably bursts. However, as I considered the photographer's perspective, I began to question whether it was truly innocence within that bubble or faith. This shift in perspective led me to consider that perhaps my life had been marked not by a loss of innocence but by a sustained absence of faith.

This thought brought me back to the previous night's encounter with Jesus. If faith wasn't fostering growth in my life, then maybe, just like in my dream, I'd been cultivating the wrong elements all along. It wasn't innocence that needed protection, but faith that needed nurturing. I'd been tending to thorns to keep others out of my garden when these were the very people who might benefit from what I could share if I allowed the divine to manifest through me.

Walking alone, I wrestled with the concept of moral injury — a term Terri, the chaplain who married Jenn and me, had once mentioned to me. Had I misunderstood her message back then? Could this be the root of my unrest? The realization that faith must play a crucial role in my healing crystallized as I neared the trailhead. It was clear that embracing faith was not just a step but a vital leap toward genuine recovery and transformation.

Emerging from the wilderness at the trailhead, I carried with me a renewed sense of purpose and a sharper perspective. The No Barriers Warriors expedition had not just tested my physical endurance; it had also provided a profound mental and emotional recalibration. This first expedition proved to be a formidable catalyst, urging me to commit to changes and challenges I had long avoided.

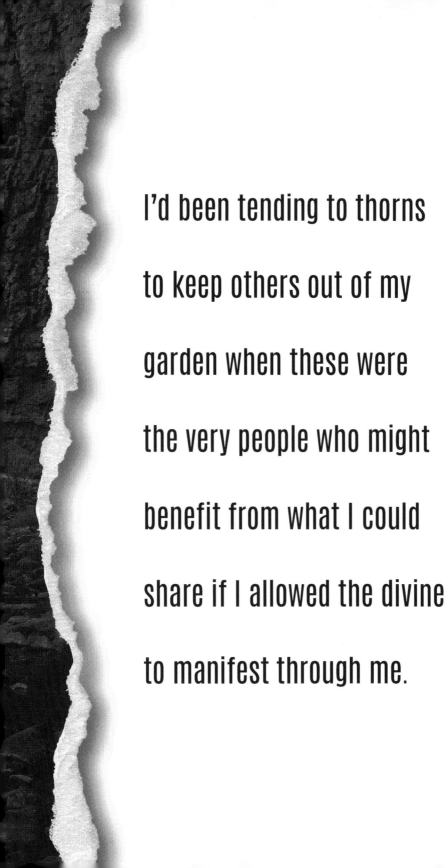

I'd been tending to thorns

to keep others out of my

garden when these were

the very people who might

benefit from what I could

share if I allowed the divine

to manifest through me.

As part of the program, each participant was encouraged to commit to a personal pledge — a challenge that would push us beyond our familiar boundaries. Reflecting on this as we traveled back to the hotel, I knew exactly what my pledge would be: I'd organize my first photography exhibition using the images I'd captured during the trip. My pledge was not just about displaying photographs; it was about demonstrating the growth I'd achieved while continuing to push myself in new and challenging directions.

This commitment was daunting because it required me to seek assistance, collaborate with others, and step away from my usual self-reliance. Additionally, by exposing my art, I would open myself up to public scrutiny and potentially harsh criticism, a prospect that had deterred me in the past. Upholding my pledge would mean reintroducing myself to the world and breaking away from the isolation I'd imposed on myself for years.

With renewed vigor and a clear path forward, I returned home noticeably transformed. The changes weren't drastic, but they were significant enough that my family could sense a shift. I embraced the pledge I'd made during the expedition, which quickly led to an invitation to participate in my first-ever photography exhibition. The show, titled *22*, was hosted at Indiana University Purdue University Indianapolis in November 2016 and focused on veteran suicide. My contributions, centered on light and darkness in landscape imagery, were displayed in stark contrast to the darker themes surrounding them. This exhibition was one of my first real engagements with the concept of moral injury, a topic seldom discussed openly.

Buoyed by the fulfillment of my pledge, I moved on to the next two No Barriers Warriors expeditions, each summit acting as a catalyst for the next challenge I'd need to overcome. By the time I was standing at more than fourteen thousand feet of elevation next to my fellow veterans at the peak of Mount Sneffels on my final Warriors trip, I realized I'd often focused too much on the destination and neglected the richness of the journey itself. There, at the summit, I vowed to relish every step of my path forward and to find joy in the journey as much as in the destination.

The year 2016 marked a significant transformational phase in my life, revealing the immense strength and resilience I possessed. I am eternally grateful for every individual I met along the way, as each played a crucial role in shaping the person I am today. The challenges I faced in that year taught me that the strength within me is sufficient to overcome any obstacle, reinforcing my gratitude and resolve to continue growing and embracing every moment of my life's path.

Chapter 9

THE POWER OF VULNERABILITY

EAGER TO MAINTAIN my momentum and stay connected with the community that had become my tribe, I jumped at the opportunity to further contribute to the No Barriers USA community. In January 2017, I was asked to represent No Barriers at a significant event to receive a donation, and I immediately accepted, not realizing the full extent of what I'd agreed to.

The event was not the small, intimate gathering I'd imagined but a major conference hosted by Prudential Retirement. For their annual kickoff that gathered all team members to strategize for the year ahead, Prudential Retirement had chosen to honor No Barriers as an organization that exemplified teamwork and collective goal achievement. My role was to accept a substantial donation and speak about the program's impact on my life in a daunting, 10-minute speech in front of more than three hundred attendees.

Despite my initial apprehension, my nerves were overshadowed by the excitement of meeting Erik Weihenmayer, cofounder of No Barriers and a man renowned for his achievements, including being the first blind person to climb Mount Everest. Arriving just hours before Erik's keynote on the first night, I was warmly welcomed, though most were unaware of my role in the event. That evening, as I entered the ballroom for dinner, unsure of where to sit and feeling out of place, I was met by Maureen, who helped ease my nerves.

Tasked with managing the event, Maureen took it upon herself to guide me through the bustling conference scene and ensured I knew my schedule, my place, and the people crucial to engage with. Her guidance was a beacon of clarity amid the overwhelming atmosphere of the event. As we walked to my designated table, she casually mentioned that I would be sitting with Erik Weihenmayer and his team — a detail that caught me off guard since I hadn't yet met him. "You'll meet Erik soon; he's preparing backstage," she reassured me before introducing me to his father, Ed, a Marine fighter pilot in Vietnam, and his wife, Ellie.

As the program started, my conversation with Ed flowed effortlessly. Despite our brief acquaintance, Ed treated me with a warm familiarity that made me feel valued and respected — an interaction that significantly boosted my confidence. I felt acknowledged not just for my past struggles but for my potential and achievements.

Watching Erik speak was exhilarating. His presence was commanding, not merely because of what he said but how he said it. His gestures, his timing, and his engagement with the audience were a well-orchestrated display. It was then that I realized the power of my own experiences and the potential to harness them into something transformative for others. Inspired, I began to see a path forward where I could use my natural inclination for storytelling and previous professional experience working in marketing and advertising to inspire and educate, much like Erik. This epiphany crystallized my desire to pursue speaking professionally and turn my journey into a vehicle for change and connection.

Rooted to my seat, absorbing every word Erik Weihenmayer spoke, I felt a profound alignment with my purpose. It dawned on me that this was the challenging path God had hinted at — one that involved tackling mental health issues publicly. Discussing mental health, especially when it pertained to conditions like PTSD or traumatic brain injuries, was fraught with misunderstandings and societal judgments. People often jump to conclusions about your capabilities and sanity, which makes being open about such personal struggles incredibly daunting. I knew sharing my experiences would open me up to such criticism, but I also knew I had an opportunity to open a dialogue about the struggles so many veterans face without alienating or frightening others. It was clear that my journey to help others would not only involve sharing my own experiences but also educating and reshaping perceptions about mental health.

After his speech, Erik made his way to our table, and I soon found myself engaged in a conversation where I shared my aspiration to photograph Mount Everest. Upon hearing this, he said, "Eric, I think that's going to be in your future. In fact, I believe whatever you decide to do can be in your future. You've overcome every challenge so far; all you have to do is believe in yourself and what you're doing.

We've always got your back here." I knew Erik wasn't just making small talk to fill the silence at the table. It felt as though he was granting me permission to pursue my ambitions, and his genuine interest in my dreams empowered me to envision a broader horizon for my life and work.

Reeling from my conversation with Erik, I returned to my hotel room for the night. His words echoed in my mind, a mantra of limitless possibilities. That night, sleep was fleeting, my mind buzzing with the potential and pathways that suddenly seemed attainable.

THE WEIGHT OF EXPECTATION

The next morning dawned with a surge of creative energy. I reshaped and refined my speech, condensing my journey and insights into a concise, 10-minute narrative. But just as I felt a sense of accomplishment, lunch with Maureen and a group of Prudential Retirement executives threw another curveball my way. Their genuine interest and enthusiasm about my story and the encouragement from Maureen led to them extending my speech to twenty minutes. Pushed into uncharted waters, my nerves were transformed into a full-blown panic.

Returning to my hotel room, the weight of expectation felt crushing. This was a closing speech for a significant corporate event, far beyond the scale of anything I'd tackled before. The room felt smaller as the clock ticked louder, each second a reminder of the rapidly approaching moment when I would stand alone before an audience of more than three hundred professionals and executives who seemed to have more faith in me than I had in myself. In a blur of fervent writing, rehearsing, and self-doubt, I crafted each sentence with a mix of fear and determination, aware that this speech could redefine my path.

When the moment finally came, stepping out onto the stage was like stepping into a new persona — one shaped by adversity but defined by resilience and hope. As I delivered each word, the initial tremble in my voice steadied. The faces in the crowd transformed from intimidating strangers into engaged listeners, their nods and attentive eyes fueling my confidence. What began as a daunting challenge morphed into a profound connection with every sentence I spoke. This speech, born of panic and pressure, became not just a recount of my journey but a testament to the very lessons of perseverance and faith I was imparting.

The response was a standing ovation, tears among the audience members, and a palpable connection that speeches rarely achieve. The impact was not fully apparent until I stepped off the stage and began navigating the line of people eager to share their stories with me; each person added a layer of validation to my journey. This experience underscored the profound power of vulnerability and the fact that sharing one's truth can transform not only the speaker but also the listener.

Shortly after my speech, I was invited to grace the cover of *VFW* magazine, an accolade that unexpectedly expanded my reach and influence. However, amid this newfound role as a speaker and advocate, I wrestled internally with feelings of inadequacy. Only a year had passed since my darkest moments, and despite the progress, I was acutely aware of the ongoing battles within.

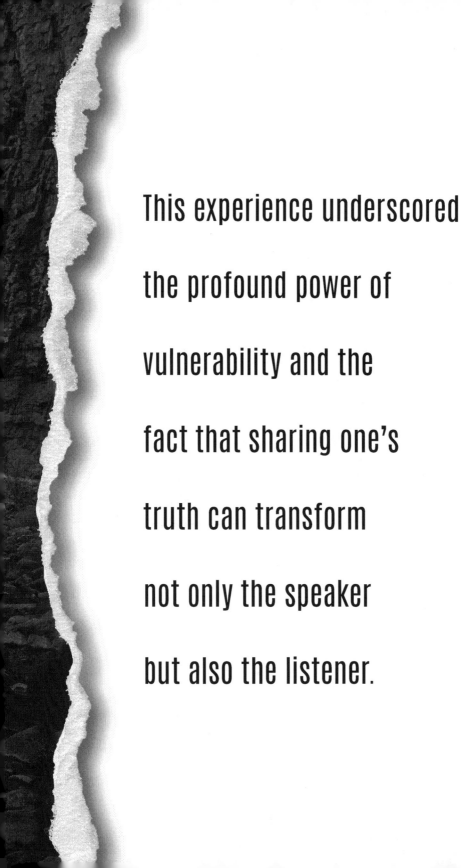

This experience underscored the profound power of vulnerability and the fact that sharing one's truth can transform not only the speaker but also the listener.

EMBRACING MY ENTREPRENEURIAL SPIRIT

In January 2017, just days after my first speech with Prudential Retirement, Maureen reached out with a proposition that intertwined my passion for photography with a new business venture. Her offer was to create thank-you gifts for all the attendees of the Prudential Retirement event where I'd just spoken. I'd need to create an eight-by-ten photo with the conference logo and the No Barriers logo included tastefully in the image. With a daunting deadline of just two and a half weeks, this project not only challenged me to establish a business on the fly but also to deliver on a large scale under tight constraints.

I knew the opportunity I'd been given wasn't a handout. It was a chance to prove myself, a hand up. Every success I'd experienced resulted in an invitation to contribute more. This realization crystalized the purpose of my business, which I decided to name Hand Up LLC — a name that reflected the essence of not merely receiving but extending a hand and giving others the chance to rise and succeed.

This initial project opened doors to more opportunities with Prudential Retirement and other firms, allowing me to furnish corporate spaces with my landscape photography and continue sharing my journey through speaking engagements. I was asked to design a series of landscapes for Prudential Retirement's office in Hartford, and by engaging with the employees about their preferences, I was able to help turn their workspace into a gallery of tranquility. Each piece was chosen to evoke serenity and inspiration, reflecting nature's ability to boost well-being.

This venture into workplace design rekindled a passion I hadn't felt in years. It wasn't just about decoration; it was about transforming environments to enhance mental and emotional health. It allowed me to merge my love for photography with my mission to improve others' lives, echoing the therapeutic impact nature had on my own recovery. Every project was a step toward healing, not just for me, but for everyone my work touched. The feedback was overwhelmingly positive, affirming that my approach could make a real difference.

As my photography business began to flourish, I was invited to participate in Prudential Retirement's VetNet, a program dedicated to supporting veteran employees. Speaking at various Prudential locations, I was struck by the number of veterans they employed and the substantial resources invested into making VetNet a supportive community for these individuals. This experience was not only humbling but also incredibly enriching, as I encouraged fellow veterans to become the best versions of themselves and fostered discussions on inclusivity and the power of vulnerability. Each successful event boosted my confidence tremendously and reminded me of the self-assurance I'd felt while serving in the military.

In May of 2017, I attended another major conference for Prudential Retirement in Naples, Florida. This time, the event was for their customers, and I was there sharing my photography and story. While in the area, I had the opportunity to reconnect with one of my dear friends, Remembrance, who arranged a dinner at an amazing little Italian restaurant where I met her husband, Joey, for the first time. But it was another dinner guest, Paulette, whose words would profoundly change the trajectory of my business and my mindset.

Paulette asked me insightful questions about my work that no one had ever asked before. She wanted to know what motivated me and what I hoped to accomplish. While most people dismissed me when I mentioned I was a landscape photographer, Paulette treated me like I was the Ansel Adams of my time. Her genuine interest made me truly listen to what she had to say.

During our conversation, I shared how I'd used some revenue from working with Prudential Retirement to rent a cabin near Rocky Mountain National Park for a weekend retreat with veterans. The goal of the trip had been to support each other in charting new paths forward, an experience that wouldn't have been possible without the revenue generated by my business. Paulette called me a philanthropist, but at first, I didn't know how to respond because I associated philanthropy with wealth. However, she explained that being a philanthropist is about giving your time and resources freely to help those around you rise. She also gave me some key pointers about what I could do to ensure my company could always give back and embody our motto, "Two are better than one; if one falls, the other is there to give a hand up."

Inspired by the wisdom of Ecclesiastes 4, the motto of Hand Up encapsulates the philosophy of mutual support that had propelled me forward in life and business. The tagline wasn't just a slogan; it reflected the real support network that had been crucial in guiding my path by providing aid, encouragement, and a chance to excel. These experiences underscored the transformative power of giving someone a hand up, not just a handout, and shaped my business's mission to uplift others as I had been uplifted.

That dinner conversation with Paulette was transformative. She gave me permission to become someone I would never have envisioned for myself. Her belief in me and her encouragement became a key ingredient in the foundation of my business and my life. Since then, I've often reflected on how remarkable it is that strangers can see things in us that we don't see in ourselves and empower us to realize our potential. I've come to believe this ability to give support so freely is the mark of a truly beautiful human being.

THREE LEGS OF A BALANCED STOOL

Photography is a passion that continuously rejuvenates my spirit and will forever be a cornerstone of my life. My portfolio is not just a collection of images; it represents a journey of personal growth and a means to connect with the breathtaking beauty of nature. However, even though photography was the catalyst for my entrepreneurial endeavors, I understood my passion for photography was only one vital leg of a stool, crucial for its emotional and aesthetic value, yet not sufficient on its own to support my broader ambitions.

Residential building and construction was the second foundational pillar of my ventures. Because I had an educational background in construction management and a few years of experience under my belt, this sector grounded my business model and offered a robust structure for revenue generation. Construction management aligned with my knack for seeing potential where others see challenges and allowed me to turn dilapidated structures into coveted homes and manage the intricacies of residential projects with precision.

In 2020, real estate brokerage became the third leg of my stool, seamlessly integrating with and complimenting my construction efforts. This synergy allowed me to provide unmatched value to clients by helping them buy, sell, and renovate properties. My comprehensive understanding of building processes enhanced my ability to advise clients beyond the standard brokerage services. From identifying promising fixer-uppers to overseeing substantial renovations, I could offer a holistic approach that reshaped traditional real estate practices and covered every aspect of property investment and management.

Together, these three disciplines form a cohesive business strategy that has propelled Hand Up LLC to significant success. The company has grown substantially, an achievement I thought unattainable when I began with just a five-hundred-dollar credit card." While my business may still be a minnow in a vast ocean, it represents a monumental personal accomplishment. And while I know most people prefer to grow quickly, I've made it a point to take my time making sure I build the right foundation that is strong enough to hold the growth and future of the company.

Beyond the financial achievements, what truly defines my entrepreneurial journey are the impacts I've been able to make along the way. From all my clients who've had increases to their net worth, to families living in their dream homes, to delivering wheelchairs to disabled children and adults in Nepal, to influencing legislation that supports veterans, and assisting Afghan refugees with essential supplies as they resettle in Indiana, each initiative has extended the reach of my enterprise beyond mere profit.

Hand Up LLC is about more than just business; it's about creating a multifaceted enterprise that supports personal growth, nurtures families, enhances communities, and will leave a legacy of which I am immensely proud. Throughout personal and global crises, including the global pandemic, my business provided a stabilizing force in my life that adapted and thrived, underscoring the resilience and flexibility I built into its core. To this day, regular breakfasts with my pastor at the pancake house keep me grounded in faith and purpose, reinforcing my commitment to using my entrepreneurial success as a platform for good.

Chapter *10*

TILL VALHALLA, BROTHER

2017 WAS FILLED with rapid growth and success, but it also brought to light the complexities of being honest and open with complete strangers about my mental health. As much as I cherished the travel and the work, the changes were bittersweet. The time away from my family was hard, but it gave me space to miss them, which, in turn, made our time together more precious. Yet, despite the accolades and outward success, I struggled. I felt like I was supposed to put forward a polished version of myself and often sidelined the ongoing struggles that come with recovery, which made me feel like I was being inauthentic. This disconnect between what I felt public expectations were and my personal truth was disconcerting and starting to bleed into my daily life.

With this balance consuming my thoughts, arriving in Alaska for Christmas that year felt like coming full circle. Not only was I returning to a place that held deep familial ties, but I was also reconnecting with Brent, the man who had been a crucial support during one of the darkest phases of my life. The anticipation of sharing these successes and new opportunities with him added an extra layer of excitement to the holiday season. As I stepped off the plane, the crisp Alaskan air felt like a refreshing new beginning. The landscape, blanketed in light snow, mirrored the clean slate I felt I was being given after a year of transformative experiences and professional growth. Brent's role in my journey had been vital, offering support from afar, and now I had the chance to update him in person on the significant strides I'd made.

I'd recently been given the opportunity to photograph an expedition in Nepal, a significant milestone, symbolizing not just professional success but also a personal victory over the adversities I had faced. Telling Brent about this upcoming adventure was a highlight of the trip. His reaction — a mix of pride and excitement — reaffirmed the profound bond of our friendship. Our reunion was filled with long conversations where we recounted the challenges and triumphs of the past year and discussed future aspirations.

Not only did I get to share my victories with Brent, but spending Christmas with my in-laws in the familiar, comforting environment of Alaska provided a well-needed respite and time to reflect. It was a reminder of how far I'd come from grappling with personal demons to standing on the brink of an exciting professional venture abroad. This holiday season was not just a celebration of traditional festivities but also a celebration of renewal and ongoing recovery, surrounded by family and friends who had been my bedrock.

THE BONDS OF FRIENDSHIP

Photographing the northern lights in Alaska had long been a goal of mine, and it seemed Christmas Day 2017 might offer the perfect opportunity. The forecast indicated the best visibility would be in Talkeetna, though reaching the town during winter presented its own set of challenges. The drive was notorious for its darkness, snow, and ice — not to mention the moose that often crossed the roads, posing a dangerous obstacle at night.

Knowing I needed a reliable companion for this nocturnal adventure, I called Brent. After checking with his wife, Amy, he said, "I can go, come pick me up." Within twenty minutes, I was at his doorstep. He hopped in with his road sodas in tow, and we set off, filled with the excitement of capturing the ethereal beauty of the auroras.

As we laughed and reminisced, it felt as though no time had passed since our last encounter. The camaraderie on that drive to Talkeetna was a reminder of our enduring friendship formed in war. However, despite the clear skies, the northern lights proved elusive, and we caught only a faint glimpse that was far from the vibrant display I'd hoped to photograph.

The return journey was less eventful in terms of celestial phenomena but became memorable for a different reason. Brent, worn out from the night's activities and perhaps the road sodas, fell asleep quickly, leaving me to navigate the dark, icy road alone. I counted more than thirty-six moose that night, each one a reminder of the dangers lurking in the Alaskan wilderness. Brent, who was supposed to help watch for them, was snoring beside me. While part of me envied his ability to sleep so soundly, I couldn't help but appreciate the solitude and the silent night around me, punctuated only by the occasional snore from my friend and the soft crunch of snow under our tires.

The next day, Brent and I opted for a climb up Flat Top Mountain just outside of Anchorage. Typically a straightforward trek, the path had transformed into a slippery ice track due to a recent rain and thaw. Equipped with crampons, we embarked on the ascent, my pace deliberately slow, not from fatigue, but from a desire to savor the camaraderie and the outdoor experience with Brent.

Reaching the summit, Brent's friends, who had joined us with plans to paraglide down, quickly took off, leaving us alone with a breathtaking vista. As we settled into the quiet of the peak, Brent turned the conversation to reflect on the past year. His question was straightforward but loaded, probing into whether I truly enjoyed my life's new trajectory. I confessed that despite the significant personal growth, I felt fraudulent promoting mental health awareness publicly while privately grappling with my own. I feared that my efforts might ultimately mean nothing, wasting time that could have been spent with my family.

Brent listened intently, offering a reflection that struck a deep chord. He shared that one of his biggest regrets was not being present for his children's formative years due to his military commitments. He dismissed the usual "You were serving your country" he received from me and others and emphasized that he'd made choices and might have prioritized differently if he knew then what he knew now. His vulnerability in acknowledging this missed opportunity highlighted the preciousness of time with loved ones, especially our children. The conversation lingered as we watched ice fog raising up from the ocean while the bright orange sun fell below the horizon, creating a spectacle of vibrant colors, marking the sky with one of God's great paintings. It was a profound moment of clarity and connection, underscored by Brent's advice to cherish and prioritize time with family above all.

Descending from the mountain, we carried the warmth of our discussion back to the cold reality, stopping for coffees to bring back to my in-laws. Brent's insights from the summit lingered, reshaping my perspective on balancing life's demands with the irreplaceable moments with loved ones. His words, a blend of regret and wisdom, were a poignant reminder of the choices we make and their long-lasting impacts.

On the day of our departure from Alaska, I realized I'd left my brand-new water bottle in Brent's truck, and we arranged to swing by his house to pick it up as we were leaving town. When we arrived, Brent greeted us warmly outside his home. He hugged Jenn affectionately and embraced the kids, handing each of them a folded piece of paper wrapped around a roll of Life Savers candy. Each paper contained the same message: "For your birthdays, your Christmases, your Valentine's — all the holidays. Take care of your mom and dad and remember your only job is to be smarter than them." Inside, there was a twenty-dollar bill for each child.

Brent knew Life Savers symbolized much more than just candy; they were a nod to my kids being my literal lifesavers, the reasons I'd stepped away from ending it all during my darkest moment. His gesture was characteristically thoughtful, albeit a bit eccentric, much like him. Our shared oddities and unwavering support for each other reminded me why we connected so deeply. I tried to hold back my emotions as I gave him a long, heartfelt hug, promising to see him when I returned in the summer for a fishing trip we planned to take together.

Upon returning home, the transition from holiday tranquility to daily routine was swift, with work commitments accelerating the passage of time. Within a day, I was absorbed in the hustle, barely noticing how quickly days turned into weeks. Then, about three weeks after leaving Alaska, I received a devastating phone call. Brent, my best friend, the very person who'd played such a crucial role in pulling me back from the brink, had taken his own life.

The shock was immediate and overwhelming. My phone slipped through my fingers and crashed to the floor. In that moment, a rush of seemingly inconsequential interactions with Brent — the Life Savers, his heartfelt hugs, his slightly cryptic messages — flashed before my eyes. It dawned on me then, with a gut-wrenching clarity, that these were not just casual gestures; they were signs I'd missed. My friend was hurting deeply, and I hadn't seen it. The realization that I'd missed the chance to offer him the same lifeline he'd extended to me was heartbreaking.

When I received the news of Brent's death, I was just hours away from boarding a plane for a significant speaking event at Prudential Retirement in Orlando, Florida. It was the same event where I'd spoken the year before, except this time, I was scheduled to present just before the keynote speaker on opening night. Despite my overwhelming grief, canceling my appearance wasn't an option.

Brent's death wasn't just a personal loss. It symbolized the fragility of my own recovery. Doubt and sorrow plagued me, eroding my confidence. By the time I arrived in Orlando, I was emotionally and physically spent. My body and mind felt close to shutting down, and I could sense old, destructive emotions resurfacing. I feared the direction I was headed and doubted my ability to speak effectively at the event.

I was on a tight schedule, and when I arrived at the hotel, I had just enough time to drop off my bags before heading to soundcheck. I quickly reviewed the key points of my speech and then returned to my room to prepare for the evening. Amid the whirlwind of preparations, I confided in Maureen, who was overseeing the event, about my loss. I felt it was crucial she understood my state of mind in case my demeanor seemed off. Despite my personal turmoil, I was determined not to let my grief detract from the evening's energy and focus on motivation and teamwork.

As I took the stage that night, I managed to suppress my emotions sufficiently to engage the audience with humor and energy. It was undoubtedly one of the most challenging speeches I've ever delivered because it demanded a display of cheerfulness and motivation that was the opposite of what I felt. I was acting the part of the enthusiastic speaker, all while wrestling with the emotional turmoil of Brent's death.

The speech went better than I had expected, maintaining the event's upbeat tone without anyone suspecting the sadness I carried. Afterward, at the networking event, I found myself on the verge of tears as Mandy Harvey stepped on stage. The lyrics of *This Time* echoed around me, amplifying a positive message of hope despite the despair I felt. As I worked to keep my composure, I was unexpectedly joined by Ed Weihenmayer.

Ed recognized my distress without needing an explanation and shared some advice that was both gentle and impactful, a timely reminder of my journey and the struggles I had overcome to be where I was. He emphasized the importance of channeling overwhelming emotions into positive actions, suggesting that the energy from my internal battles could transform into something beneficial, not just for myself but for those around me. This conversation reinforced the concept of the ripple effect, a principle I'd previously discussed with his son, Erik. Ed's advice to transform negative ripples into waves of positivity, coupled with a reassuring hug, left a lasting impression. As Ed departed, I sat there processing the powerful idea that my personal turmoil could be redirected to create positive impacts in the world, turning my pain into a force for good.

Carrying Ed's advice and the lyrics of Mandy's song, I realized the storm of grief I was experiencing because of Brent's death could wreak havoc in my life if I allowed it. The clarity of hindsight makes it easy to recognize patterns and missed opportunities painfully clear, and I knew my historical coping mechanisms were damaging to both me and those I loved. This moment of reflection about my previous tendencies and Brent's death underscored a profound truth about combating suicide: the most potent weapon against despair is hope. The hope that things can improve is a lifeline we can offer by sharing our struggles openly, admitting when we're not okay, and accepting the support needed to pave the way for healing.

The hope that things can improve is a lifeline we can offer by sharing our struggles openly, admitting when we're not okay, and accepting the support needed to pave the way for healing.

Every day, the memory of Brent weighs on me, a reminder of the impact his life and tragic departure have had not only on me but also on his wife, his boys, and all his friends and their families. We are all flawed, navigating our imperfections as best we can. Brent was no exception. In the face of his challenges, he offered me hope and guidance, a gift I desperately wish I could have reciprocated. Brent's legacy teaches me the importance of being present, of really listening, and of offering support not just in moments of crisis but consistently, as a bulwark against the dark times. It's a lesson about the power of vulnerability and the importance of connection, one that I carry forward in his memory, hoping to offer the same support to others that he once gave to me.

Chapter *11*

LOOK FOR THE HELPERS

WAVES OF POSITIVITY

THE WEIGHT OF grief and stress had taken a physical toll on me, and when I returned home, I was on the brink of hospitalization. I negotiated with my doctors to manage my treatment from home, understanding the delicate balance between self-care and medical necessity. It was a critical juncture because, without a proactive change to my physical health, I was at risk of undoing all the progress I'd made.

As I began healing at the beginning of 2018, I focused on my upcoming expedition to Nepal. The trip, organized by Heather Thomson of *The Real Housewives of New York*, included a significant visit to the Center for Disabled Children Assistance (CDCA). This center, a non-governmental organization dedicated to creating equal opportunities for disabled children in society, seemed like the perfect opportunity to apply the principle of transforming negative ripples into positive waves.

In preparation for the trip, I communicated with Dendi, the founder of CDCA, to understand the center's needs. Expecting a list of toys or clothes, I was surprised when he said they urgently needed eight wheelchairs. This request posed a unique challenge, as Nepal lacked the facilities to purchase wheelchairs locally. Conflicted and overwhelmed, I sought advice from Jenn, who reminded me of the importance of taking care of myself as I healed and not taking on too much. However, feeling compelled to participate in this endeavor, I said, "If we feel like we are being called to help, aren't we supposed to respond? Isn't that what faith is?"

Jenn's agreement was all I needed to message Dendi and commit to providing the wheelchairs despite not knowing how to accomplish the task.

My commitment to the CDCA and the children it served was not just about aid; it was a pivotal moment of choosing faith, hope over despair, and action over inaction. It was a testament to the belief that even in our darkest moments, we can find the strength to light the way for others and turn personal trials into transformative victories.

When I said I'd deliver eight wheelchairs to Nepal, I had no idea how to start, but I knew I needed to act. My first call was to Heather to inform her of my pledge. Her enthusiasm and support sparked a chain reaction, and everyone I reached out to offered to help. Erik Weihenmayer introduced me to Wayne Hanson, whose organization, ROC Wheels, delivers wheelchairs to developing countries. Wayne not only agreed to provide the wheelchairs but also arranged for a specialist to travel to Nepal to train local staff on their maintenance and fitting.

The fundraising target was eleven thousand dollars, and through my network, I quickly raised the first seven thousand. But, as the short deadline approached, I feared I might not meet the goal. Heather, understanding the urgency, tapped into her resources and filled the gap. Her generosity to help was overwhelming and ensured that the wheelchairs would reach those in need.

After securing funding, the physical chairs, and the support of specialists, I had to tackle the daunting logistic challenges. With just twenty-four hours before my flight, I had no plan for transporting the wheelchairs to Nepal. In a last-ditch effort, I rented a truck and drove the wheelchairs to Chicago, storing them at the Hilton attached to the airport. The next day, with the help of a porter at O'Hare who knew exactly who to speak to at the airline, the wheelchairs were checked in without charge.

Sitting on the plane, I felt a profound sense of accomplishment. What had seemed insurmountable weeks earlier had been achieved through the collective efforts of friends, strangers, and professionals who all shared a commitment to making a difference. This experience was not just about delivering wheelchairs but about community, connection, and turning a personal tragedy into a positive ripple that extended far beyond my own life. It was also about growing my faith. Upon landing, we were met by Dendi and our guides, who assisted us in transporting the wheelchairs to the CDCA. Now, the real work began.

Over the next two days, we assembled the eight wheelchairs and carefully fitted each child. What struck me most during the fitting sessions was not just the children's joy but the profound relief and gratitude expressed by

What had seemed

insurmountable weeks

earlier had been achieved

through the collective

efforts of friends, strangers,

and professionals who all

shared a commitment to

making a difference.

their parents. Many of these children had conditions like cerebral palsy that made mobility a significant challenge. Parents, especially mothers, had to carry their children everywhere. These wheelchairs meant freedom and safety for their children and relief from the physical strain they had endured for years. The depth of their gratitude was moving and humbling, truly emphasizing the impact of our efforts.

Though still mourning his passing, I envisioned Brent, always the protector and caretaker, joyously interacting with children in wheelchairs, echoing the love and laughter he shared with his own family and mine. This vision reinforced my commitment to fostering meaningful change and highlighted the undeniable power of community and compassion in overcoming global challenges.

Unfortunately, just as we were wrapping up our work at the CDCA, I began to feel unwell. At first, I dismissed it as physical and emotional exhaustion from the last couple of days at the CDCA, but I soon realized it was something more serious. I rushed to the bathroom, overcome by sudden nausea and diarrhea, signaling the start of a physical reaction I hadn't anticipated.

The complications of my illness struck me hard during the second night of our stay in Nepal. Initially assuming it was bad gut bacteria, I started treatment with Cipro, but my condition only worsened. With severe symptoms preventing my planned flight to Lukla, I stayed back, hoping for a quick recovery. By the third day, however, my fever soared up to one hundred and four degrees, and I was barely coherent, lost in a fog of sickness.

It was in the haze of this illness that I checked my email and discovered an invitation from the Iraq and

Afghanistan Veterans of America (IAVA) to become a leadership fellow, a program focused on shaping policies on Capitol Hill, influencing laws, and ensuring that veterans' voices were heard and accounted for. Although I felt fulfilled with my current project, I was intrigued by the idea of pursuing a form of advocacy with the potential to reshape veterans' lives at a systemic level. My excitement at the invitation and ability to accept the role within their established timeline gave a boost to my mental state as I struggled through my illness.

That evening, the owner of our guide company, a veteran of the British military, visited me and urgently suggested I return home for medical care. Taking his advice to heart, I contacted Jenn, who swiftly arranged a change in my flights. Jenn met me when my flight landed in Chicago, and we immediately opted to drive home rather than stay in Chicago. Given my deteriorating condition, we suspected I would be hospitalized, and I wanted to be close to home for Jenn and the kids' sake.

At Saint Vincent's Hospital in Carmel, Indiana, the seriousness of my situation was immediately apparent. Imaging revealed that my colon was nearly bursting due to my use of Imodium to manage my symptoms during travel. Diagnosed with an antibiotic-resistant form of salmonella, which had caused extensive ulceration throughout my colon, I faced an eight-day hospital stay followed by weeks of IV antibiotic treatments.

Despite the physical pain and the intensity of the situation, I felt a profound sense of accomplishment. And by staying in touch with Dendi and his team, I learned about their resourceful efforts to expand their mission beyond our initial contribution. They were scouring landfills for salvageable wheelchairs, repairing broken ones, and finding ways to equip more children and adults with mobility aids. Their dedication inspired me to deepen my involvement, leading to a partnership with the Wheelchair Foundation.

Collaborating with the Wheelchair Foundation and Wayne from ROC Wheels, I embarked on a new project to help Dendi establish a more permanent wheelchair repair and distribution center in Nepal. Given the country's challenging terrain and remote locations, delivering aid was complex and costly. However, our joint efforts paid off, and as of Memorial Day 2024, more than nine hundred wheelchairs have been shipped to the center, which has become a pivotal institution in Nepal for those in need of mobility aids. Now, the center operates independently and is one of the preferred destinations for wheelchair donations within the country.

By June of 2018, I found myself in Washington, DC, diving into the world of veteran advocacy. It was a new passion fueled by the desire to enact real change. Over the next six years, this role opened my eyes to how our government works and what it takes to get something passed into law. The number of skills and lessons I have learned during this time has been invaluable, both personally and professionally. I participated in discussions at the forefront, helping to pass into law five major pieces of legislation that help veterans, including two that hold deep personal significance: the 988 Suicide Hotline Act and the PACT Act.

The 988 Suicide Hotline Act created a lifeline for those who might not have a support system, like Brent was for me, in their darkest moments. This law means that there is always someone ready to help on the other side of the call. The PACT Act addresses the health issues veterans face due to exposure to toxins, like the burn pits that likely contributed to my own severe thyroid problems and autoimmune issues. This legislation ensures that veterans wouldn't have to fight to prove the impact of their sacrifices on their health. It is an acknowledgement and an assurance from the nation we served that says, "We see what you gave, and we will take care of you."

The 988 Suicide Hotline Act and the PACT Act are more than just professional achievements; they are a testament to what can be accomplished when you channel personal trials into advocacy for broader change. Despite the exhaustion of repeated trips to DC and the frustration of pushing against bureaucratic resistance, every new challenge confirmed the need for continued advocacy. Each time I considered stepping away, a new need arose, reaffirming my commitment.

Looking back, if I hadn't been sick in Nepal, I would have missed the email inviting me to join IAVA and the deadline to apply for the fellowship program. I always tell my children that when we get what we want, it's God's direction, and when we don't get what we want, it's God's protection. This situation is a perfect example of God closing a door on one opportunity and opening a window to another.

At the time, being sick felt like the worst situation imaginable because I couldn't realize my dream of photographing Mount Everest. However, had I been on the mountain, I would have missed out on the amazing opportunity to work with IAVA and so many amazing individuals who

The 988 Suicide Hotline Act and the PACT Act are more than just professional achievements; they are a testament to what can be accomplished when you channel personal trials into advocacy for broader change.

changed my life and its trajectory while making a difference in the community I dearly love.

My service, both abroad and at home, taught me that serving others is a vital method for coping with personal struggles. Whether it was helping kids in Nepal or advocating for fellow veterans in the US, focusing on others provided a respite from my inner turmoil. Serving others was a powerful antidote to the introspective cycle of despair. It not only provided aid but also enriched my life, echoing the ethos Mr. Rogers championed about finding the helpers. In times of personal crisis, becoming a helper myself has been both a lifeline and a pathway to healing.

Chapter *12*

FAREWELL FORTY-FOUR

IN THE LATE fall of 2005, I left Charlie Company and joined the scout sniper platoon of our battalion. The platoon was made up of a diverse group of thirty Type-A individuals and allowed me to expand my connections within the battalion. One of the strongest bonds I formed was with a man named Dustin. A towering figure and avid gym rat, Dustin, like me, freely expressed his frustrations with military inefficiencies yet took his duties seriously. We quickly became good friends, especially after I discovered I was just six days older than him — a fact he relished as it made me the "grandpa" of our platoon instead of him.

In Iraq, Dustin became a key ally. We often dined together at the chow halls and seized any chance to collaborate on tasks. I was part of the headquarters element, working with various squads, while Dustin led Squad Three. His companionship helped ease the monotony and challenges of deployment. We shared endless discussions critiquing the Army's shortcomings, yet paradoxically, we both held deep-seated respect for serving and loved it to our core.

Dustin's loyalty was unwavering, a defining trait that solidified his status as one of my best friends. After our return stateside, we continued to work together closely. While I awaited my transfer to the Warrior Transition Program, I served as the NCOIC of our Headquarters Company, and Dustin temporarily led the scout sniper platoon during its leadership transition. This period allowed us to maintain daily interactions, sharing meals and experiences as we navigated the transitions within our platoon.

It wasn't long before Dustin moved out of Alaska, and shortly after, I moved into the Warrior Transitions Unit, where I would eventually retire. Despite our geographical separation, I took pride in watching Dustin excel as he moved on to the Green to Gold program and became a respected officer. However, even though his career flourished, like me, Dustin tended to suppress his struggles, choosing anger over vulnerability. This coping mechanism, so familiar to both of us, was just one of the ways we shared an intrinsic understanding of each other's lives and battles.

Before the story of my mental health struggles and suicide attempt became public through a *VFW* magazine feature and other outlets, I confided in Dustin privately. I knew he would empathize with my experience, but I didn't anticipate the depth of the connection this revelation would foster between us. Revealing my struggles unexpectedly opened a channel for him to share his own battles that echoed the very issues I'd faced. The critical difference, however, was his active-duty status. Dustin felt that seeking help could jeopardize his military career, a reality many service members painfully navigate.

After my conversation with Dustin, I reached out to Brent for support, who insightfully reminded me that while he was always there for Dustin, this time, Dustin needed *me*. Brent encouraged me to pay it forward, asserting that I was ready to be the support Dustin needed, just as he had been for me.

Hearing Brent's confident words about my role in Dustin's life, I felt the weight of responsibility settle onto my shoulders. Even though Brent's words were encouraging, I grappled with self-doubt. Reflecting on Alex Hormozi's notion that "you outwork your self-doubt by creating an undeniable stack of proof that you are who you say you are," I feared my accomplishments and growth were insufficient to guide Dustin effectively. This fear of failing him loomed large, challenging my readiness to support a friend in dire need.

PAYING IT FORWARD

Filled with battles, lessons, and triumphs, Dustin's story mirrored my own. We were just men striving to become better than our pasts as we grappled with the complexities of life. When Dustin first confided in me about his struggles, I knew telling him what he should or shouldn't do wasn't the right approach. This method had never worked for me, and I knew it wouldn't work for him either. Instead, I made sure to be present and supportive by taking his calls or calling him back as soon as I could, even if just for a brief chat. Often, calls were made just to share a laugh over a silly joke, but it was our commitment to each other that truly mattered.

However, life, as it does, continued to test Dustin. Personal loss, marital strife, and the many pressures of work commitments were all formidable challenges, but it was the harsh, unexpected blows that threatened to drag him back into old military habits of channeling frustration into anger. Throughout these struggles, I hoped to keep Dustin from reaching what I called the "kitchen table moment" — a personal crisis like the one I'd experienced. Despite my efforts, he found himself at that breaking point. Thankfully, by the grace of God and with the support of his amazing sister, family, and many others, including myself, Dustin navigated through those dark times successfully.

It's a harsh reality that in the military, such moments of vulnerability are often seen as a weakness and viewed through a lens of judgment rather than understanding. However, hitting rock bottom became a turning point for Dustin, leading him to seek the help he needed and guiding him toward retirement and a new chapter in life. Dustin's journey, fraught with personal battles and societal judgments, underscores the complexity of mental health issues among veterans. It's a reminder of the critical need for empathy, support, and a reevaluation of how mental health is perceived in high-stress environments like the military or first responders.

BEING A SHEEPDOG

Dustin's return to civilian life was a testament to the resilience that defined him. After being separated from his children for a long stretch, he was ecstatic about reuniting

It's a harsh reality

that in the military,

such moments of

vulnerability are often

seen as a weakness

and viewed through a

lens of judgment rather

than understanding.

with them. He also loved getting to hang out with his amazing sister and her family, especially his nieces. He called his time with them Uncle Dustin's Daycare. Like me, Dustin often presented as a curmudgeon — a facade that masked our mutual apprehension about opening up after past hurts. Despite his gruff exterior, Dustin was a big softie at heart. He quickly landed a job and threw himself into the work with the same dedication he did while serving. This job, combined with a newfound love interest and his passion for softball, shaped a seemingly content life for him.

It wasn't until June 2021 that Dustin and I had a profound conversation where he unexpectedly opened up about his lack of contentment and the loss of a sense of purpose he felt from his days in the military and as a police officer. Then, he asked a question he said he thought might upset me.

"Why you?" he asked.

He wondered why it was my story, among so many potent veteran stories, that was highlighted in the news and on Capitol Hill. This question echoed one my brother had asked in 2017 when I'd appeared on the cover of *VFW* magazine. Initially, my brother's question had angered me because I thought he was belittling my experiences. However, because of how much growth I'd experienced since then, when Dustin asked, I realized they both only sought to understand.

This time, I responded with laughter instead of anger. I explained to Dustin that the visibility I'd received wasn't due to the uniqueness of my story or my personal specialness. Rather, it was because I was willing to share openly and expose the lessons I'd learned in hopes of helping others in similar predicaments. I explained that being a sheepdog, a protector in God's service, doesn't always involve physical confrontations or carrying a gun. Sometimes, it's about offering guidance from behind the scenes. It's about sharing one's narrative to prevent others from making the same missteps and from facing the same dark moments alone.

By sharing our stories, we not only free ourselves but also foster change and provide hope for others. I stressed to Dustin the importance of approaching the opportunity to share our stories not as a showcase of valor but as a beacon for those still struggling in silence. The uncomfortable conversations, the discourse around veterans' struggles, and the vulnerability required to share your truth, can deter others from a path that leads to irrevocable decisions that rob their families of their presence and steal the beauty and purpose of their lives. In these moments of shared truths, the only loser is despair itself. After conveying this to Dustin, I let the silence hang, giving him the space to digest the gravity of our exchange.

Dustin was surprised at my response, so I reiterated the impact his story could have. "Dustin, your story could change lives. It could resonate with veterans who see themselves in you. There are ways to do that and still pay the bills," I said.

There was another moment of silence before he responded, "Eric, let's do it. I want to help. I'm not sure how all this looks or what's involved, but I feel like I can make a difference."

"I don't just feel it, Dustin; I know you can," I replied, my voice thick with conviction. "And I'd love to figure out how

Being a sheepdog, a protector in God's service, doesn't always involve physical confrontations or carrying a gun. Sometimes, it's about offering guidance from behind the scenes.

we can tour this country together, sharing a message of hope and resilience. If we could be that beacon of light for even one person, who knows what they might go on to achieve?"

As excited as I was to bring this new venture to life, I wanted to make sure he understood what he was getting himself into. I said, "When you decide to share your story, there will be naysayers. People who will downplay your experiences are often those who haven't yet found healing themselves. But I can't think of anyone better to join forces with to try and create positive change."

Dustin's enthusiasm grew as we brainstormed. "What are you thinking? Getting an RV and traveling around doing that sort of thing?" he asked.

"That's exactly what I've dreamed of," I admitted. "Buying an RV to see America in a way I haven't before and flying in my kids to see the most incredible parts of the US. But more than that, I want to share our journey from the road and spread the idea that it's possible to find light and change your circumstances."

Dustin and I were both excited about this new venture, but more importantly, I was thrilled Dustin recognized the influence his story could wield in changing others' lives. In the weeks that followed, our planning took a more practical turn. We exchanged messages about RVs and discussed other logistics, like accommodating dogs and motorcycles. Dustin's enthusiasm was infectious and pushed me to commit to a long-held aspiration of mine.

"You know, I've always wanted to get my motorcycle license and a Harley," I told him.

"Fuck, yes, you need to do it, especially if we're hitting the road together," he challenged.

"Fuck, okay," I agreed, excited by the prospect of this new adventure we were plotting. Our shared path was not just about revisiting the landscapes of America but about rewriting our narratives and potentially transforming the lives of others who might see themselves in our stories.

As July drew to a close, Dustin called and told me he tore a muscle in his groin during a softball game. He'd always had a nothing's-going-to-hold-me-back mentality, and although he complained to me about the pain, he kept pushing himself hard despite advice to take it easy. On the evening of August 2, 2021, Dustin sent me a message saying he felt unwell. Our lighthearted conversation shifted quickly when he told me he'd gone to the VA emergency room. They'd sent him home, but he still felt like he was struggling to breathe. I spent the night worrying about him, feeling unsettled by what he'd shared.

The next morning, I checked in to see if he felt better, but there was no response. I assumed he was sleeping and dove into the day's work. It wasn't until later that afternoon that I received a message from his sister informing me that Dustin had passed away in the night. The details around his death weren't immediately clear, but from what I gathered, his heart had simply given out.

Losing Dustin was a stark reminder of the fragility of life and the importance of the conversations and plans we'd been making about sharing our stories to help others. His sudden departure was not only a personal tragedy but also a call to honor his memory by continuing our mission to spread hope and resilience.

Dustin was the last person I'd openly shared everything with, like the details of my marriage, my deepest thoughts, and my feelings. Despite the profound sadness and the void his passing has left, I understand he is at peace now. Dustin might have appeared tough and unyielding on the outside, but in truth, he was a soft-hearted man who contributed positively to the lives of everyone he knew and even those he didn't. Not a day goes by that I don't think of him, much like I think of Brent. Though I've switched phones a few times since losing both Brent and Dustin, I find myself unable to delete their contacts. Doing so feels like acknowledging their finality in a way I'm not yet ready to accept.

LESSONS LEARNED FROM LOSS

Dustin was the forty-fourth friend from the military I've lost, a tally that reflects a wide range of connections. Some were acquaintances from my time in Washington, DC; others were comrades from basic training, Airborne School, and all my former units. Still others were veterans I met through various programs. The sobering reality of having lost forty-four people — each of whom I cared about, wished the best for, and shared at least one positive memory with — is a staggering weight to bear. Not a month passes without a painful anniversary and a reminder of someone I've lost. These recollections of laughter, camaraderie, trust, and mutual respect aren't just memories; they are reminders of relationships that took time and shared experiences to build. They represent a network of trust and support, painfully thinned over the years. The grief that accompanies these memories is profound, tied to the joy once shared and the void their passing has left.

After Dustin passed, I stopped keeping count of the number of friends I'd lost. To continue seemed futile, as if I were merely adding marks to a tally of losses that already felt overwhelming. Similarly, after Brent, I stopped counting the friends who took their own lives, even though I know the number has surpassed nineteen. Each loss, each name added to these grim lists, represents a different type of breaking point in my life, teaching me new lessons in grief, resilience, and the value of the time we share.

Here are some lessons that losing so many friends has taught me:

Mortality and Purpose: We are all going to die. We are not meant for eternity; rather, we are given one chance to discover and share the gifts God has bestowed upon us.

Handling Life's Challenges: Life is filled with problems and will never slow down or become easier as we age. What matters is our response. Choosing to react in ways that spread love and allow God's light to shine through us is key to finding happiness amid chaos.

Coping with Disappointment and Grief: Disappointment and grief are inevitable parts of life. The question is, how do we handle them? Do we suppress our feelings, react with anger, or channel these emotions into something positive?

Finding Goodness: To navigate through grief and live a fulfilling life, it's essential to consistently find the goodness in the human spirit. This requires a strong faith to see the potential for good in such circumstances — especially during the loss of a loved one.

The Continuity of Grief: Grief never eases nor disappears. We will always miss those who were significant in our lives and yearn for their presence. The challenge is to see death not just as an end but as a transformation where physical absence is supplanted by a spiritual presence that endures through us.

Spiritual Presence: I've come to realize that our loved ones' spirits manifest around us — whether through the blooming of flowers, the birds at our window, or the sunset that recalls a shared moment. Acknowledging this has made my grief more manageable. Now, I openly converse with those I've lost, expressing my feelings out loud without concern for others' judgments. These conversations, though one-sided, often provide the insights I yearn for.

Living Promises: Following Dustin's passing, I kept my promises. I got my motorcycle endorsement and bought my first Harley. Riding makes me feel closer to him, as if he's right there with me. We had plans to share our stories together, and while I can't speak for him, I can share mine and the parts where our lives intertwined. Our bond and the impact of our friendship persist beyond his physical presence. And this book is a step in keeping that promise as well.

Through these reflections, and by being an alchemist, I've embraced the losses and transformed my approach to grief and remembrance in a way that allows me to still feel connected and close to those I miss while thriving in the present and into the future, not looking backward at what I have lost. Additionally, by sharing these stories, I illuminate paths for others, offering glimpses of hope and resilience. The journey of sharing is not just about coping with loss but also about celebrating the continuous influence of those who have passed.

The journey of sharing

is not just about coping

with loss but also

about celebrating the

continuous influence of

those who have passed.

Chapter *13*

ROAD TO RESILIENCE

IT'S IMPORTANT TO point out that it's not just external life events that can drive a person to their own "kitchen table moment." Your mental response to poor physical health and trauma also plays a role in your overall well-being. In 2008, I moved into the Warrior Transition Unit and began therapy for the traumatic brain injuries that were causing me to struggle to speak and organize my thoughts, as well as treatment for PTSD and physical issues related to my back and neck. Initially, I felt fortunate that my problems seemed minor compared to what many veterans endure. Despite my private discontent about my future, I was grateful for the support and threw myself into the therapies.

I credit the unwavering support provided by my circle for my recovery and independence. No one, not my nurse case manager, my wife, nor my mother, ever allowed me to use my disabilities as an excuse. They insisted on the opposite approach, often reminding me not to see my disabilities as a barrier.

"Don't use your disabilities as an excuse. Many others face far greater challenges than you," they would say. And they were right. Because of their perspective, I never felt sorry for myself. I believed recovery was not only possible but likely and that the only limits I faced were the ones I created through the stories I told myself.

Progress in therapy brought me some peace, and I felt well-equipped for life post-retirement. I dove into landscaping and construction projects with vigor, but in 2014, my condition took a downturn. Pain began shooting down my shins and spreading across my body. These episodes were unpredictable and debilitating. The initial medical responses were dismissive, attributing the pain to existing conditions like herniated discs or previous kidney stones. However, the pain persisted and spread, leading to frequent emergency room visits without a definitive diagnosis.

By 2015, I was in constant pain, leading to weight gain and depression. Despite the myriad of doctors involved, no one could pinpoint the cause. That year, after moving to Indiana, a rheumatologist diagnosed me with Fibromyalgia, a mysterious autoimmune condition that manifests as widespread pain and fatigue. The diagnosis was both a relief and a frustration. My condition finally had a label, but little in the way of a clear path to improvement.

The theory that environmental exposures during my service in Iraq might have triggered my condition seemed plausible to my doctors, though unprovable. This possibility added to my frustration and the complexity of managing my health. I was also diagnosed with Hashimoto's disease, which attacks the thyroid, adding another layer to my health challenges. Additional health issues like an enlarged prostate, herniated discs, and deteriorating joints compounded my difficulties. Each new diagnosis felt like a setback, yet it also clarified the extent of my physical struggles. Recognizing the need for significant lifestyle changes, I revamped my diet and focused more intently on my physical health, paralleling my ongoing efforts to improve my mental and spiritual well-being.

A HOLISTIC APPROACH TO HEALTH

I eventually realized that traditional medications like tramadol, while helpful in managing pain, sapped my motivation and carried a stigma that I found didn't represent me or who I was. This realization led me to seek alternative treatments and adopt a holistic approach to my health by integrating physical, mental, and spiritual practices. However, because of my extensive medical history, every interaction with a medical professional required a delicate approach to communication to avoid overwhelming them with the complexities of my many conditions while still ensuring effective treatment. Understanding the deep connections between my physical condition and my overall well-being was about more than just managing my symptoms; it was about striving to live a full life despite chronic conditions.

I decided to test this new approach with a massage therapist I hoped would be able to address the scar tissue in my abdomen. It resulted from surgery to remove a recalled kugel mesh implant I'd struggled with for nearly a decade. The massage therapist was remarkable and introduced me to a form of Mayan abdominal massage that helped alleviate my discomfort. And, because of my choice to seek additional alternative care and carefully communicate my medical history, the massage therapist recommended Vitalize Physical Therapy where two doctors were pivotal in addressing multiple issues with my back, neck, hips, and enlarged prostate through methods like dry needling and pelvic floor therapy.

The Vitalize team developed a personalized plan combining exercise and a daily routine to maintain my health off opioids and advance my recovery. Through them, I was introduced to a functional health nurse practitioner, who revolutionized the way I view and manage my health. The nurse practitioner guided me through an elimination diet, which, despite its challenges, was enlightening. I cut out red meat and other triggers that exacerbated my symptoms, significantly reducing inflammation and flare-ups.

Working with the physical therapists and nurse practitioner has allowed me to improve my health significantly and eliminate pain medicines all together. Although I've encountered several plateaus that required us to reassess and adjust my treatment plans and supplements. I've kept a positive mindset, accepted the changes, and pushed forward."

Even with the significant progress I'd made with my health, in the spring of 2022, a cold snap caused me to slip on an icy patch in our driveway, resulting in another traumatic brain injury that required extensive treatment for both a concussion and injuries to my jaw. During this period, scans of my head and neck revealed a nodule in the center of my thyroid, which was initially deemed non-threatening compared to the concussion and its immediate needs. Focusing on recovering from my concussion, I underwent additional physical therapy for my brain and jaw, but my health continued to decline, and I unexpectedly lost more weight, dropping below one hundred and fifty pounds.

I was fortunate to meet my current endocrinologist at a critical time. Despite her busy schedule, I was able to get in rather quickly based on my nurse practitioner's referral. The endocrinologist was chosen because of her background and work she'd done at Boston University, particularly in relation to environmental pollutants and their effects on the endocrine system. By the time of my appointment, my weight had plummeted to a gaunt one hundred and thirty-five pounds. I appeared sickly, which heightened my anxiety about my health, and the endocrinologist didn't waste any time searching for a diagnosis. Upon seeing me, she ordered a biopsy of the thyroid nodule that had been discovered. Despite my fear of long needles, we proceeded with the biopsy, which returned a precancerous result. This meant the tumor wasn't fully benign but had the potential to develop into cancer.

Given these results, the endocrinologist connected me with a new primary care doctor who decided a PET scan was necessary. The scan confirmed the presence of cancer within the thyroid, and it became clear my thyroid needed to be removed. I was referred to an amazing surgeon, whose empathy and professionalism made the process less daunting. I am profoundly grateful for her skill and care, as well as for the support from her whole team.

This series of health crises underscores the importance of holistic care and proactive communication in managing complex health issues. It's a testament to the necessity of understanding one's body and the critical role of health professionals who not only treat but truly collaborate with their patients.

CHOOSING PROACTIVE LIVING

After my thyroidectomy, I was unprepared for the profound impact the loss of my thyroid would have on my endocrine system and hormones. Within seventy-two hours, a darkness clouded over the positivity I'd once felt, and my mood fluctuated intensely. By the third night after my surgery, I realized this disruption was leading me back toward suicidal thoughts — a space I thought I had long since navigated away from. Fortunately, years before, understanding the dangerous potential of these dark thoughts after my "kitchen table moment," I'd crafted an action plan to counteract a downward spiral. That night, I confided in Jenn about my struggles, emphasizing the connection to my surgery and the upheaval it caused in my body.

We made it through the weekend, and first thing on Monday, I was in my primary care doctor's office, executing the emergency plan I'd never hoped to use. The rapid response with medications helped stabilize me, and I was profoundly thankful for having put a plan in place to bring me back from the edge. Throughout 2023, as I adjusted to life without a thyroid, I faced numerous trials within my business and personal life that made me feel like I was going backward and losing the momentum I'd gained in the years prior, but I refused to quit moving forward. By the end of the year, I realized that making my physical health a priority alongside my family and my faith had led me to a healthier place, both emotionally and physically.

I understand the pain and frustration of having unresolved health issues, of feeling misunderstood and doubted. I know the isolation of not being able to pursue your passions. I've made tough decisions to forgo certain joys to maintain my well-being, prioritizing my role as a father and ensuring I'm there for my children every day. As I've navigated my physical health struggles post-deployment, I've faced the temptation to dwell on my injuries and the limitations they imposed, to sink into a victim mentality and believe that nothing is fair, and life is unbearably hard. However, I chose a different narrative. I focused on where I wanted to go, asking God to illuminate my path or shield me, accepting any outcome as His will. This mindset shift from victimhood to proactive living still shapes my life's direction.

And it hasn't just been my physical health that has required continuous attention. The vital connection between our mental and physical health is a link I've experienced intimately. Despite grappling with significant health issues, I've realized the power I hold to mitigate their impact through mental health management. In my experience, mental resilience isn't built in therapy sessions alone. Those meetings, while incredibly important, often felt more passive than proactive. Instead, I've realized cultivating positive mental health is about taking action and being engaged in life, especially when physical ailments sideline us from activities we love.

Furthermore, my journey of resilience involves understanding and managing long-term health implications like

Chronic Traumatic Encephalopathy (CTE), a condition more recognized in NFL players but equally pertinent to military veterans like me. Having survived multiple IEDs and other incidents resulting in brain injuries, the long-term effects on my cognitive function are undeniable. Through consultations with a neurologist who specializes in CTE, I've learned about the potential for future complications and the importance of proactive brain health management, including good hydration, nutrition, and avoiding alcohol, which exacerbates the effects of traumatic brain injuries.

In essence, managing these challenges isn't just about dealing with the immediate effects but also preparing for the long-term implications on both my physical presence and mental health. It's about making informed choices that prioritize my well-being and allow me to be there for my family — the central focus of my legacy and joy.

In sharing the details of my physical and mental health challenges, my intention isn't to evoke sympathy or to suggest I've had it worse than others — quite the opposite. Traveling across the country, I've met countless veterans and community members, each with their own profound stories of struggle. These encounters, often filled with tales of unimaginable hardship, have deeply humbled me. Despite their challenges, these individuals exuded resilience and joy, greeting me with smiles that belied their personal sorrows. Meeting and talking with other veterans like them has reinforced the powerful lesson that there is always someone facing tougher trials, a reality I accept not with resentment but with profound respect.

A common thread among these inspiring individuals is a robust foundation of faith. This faith doesn't just buoy them during the storm; it enables them to cherish the calm and truly appreciate moments of peace and connection, however fleeting. My prayers once focused on seeking relief from pain and a return to my former health. However, inspired by the incredible people I've met, my prayers have transformed. Now, I ask for resilience to emulate their strength and for the grace to let my own light shine through to bring laughter, positivity, and support to others. This prayer has allowed me to become not only stronger but also more empathetic and a better father, husband, and entrepreneur.

Chronic illness can easily narrow our perspective and cause us to dwell on our suffering. Yet, I've observed that those who endure the most are often the most grateful, forgiving, and content. They've taught me the power of gratitude and the strength that comes from enduring. To anyone struggling: remember, you are not alone. Whatever goals or dreams you hold, keep reaching. Even if your aspirations seem as distant as the moon, striving toward them ensures you'll land among the stars, surrounded by the light of possibilities.

Chronic illness can easily narrow our perspective and cause us to dwell on our suffering. Yet, I've observed that those who endure the most are often the most grateful, forgiving, and content.

Chapter *14*

ANCHORED IN FAITH

IN 2015, I tried to end a life I'd come to despise and hate. The weight of my world was unbearable, and I felt trapped in a cycle of darkness and pain. My suffering was compounded by the irrevocable harm I'd caused by letting anger dominate my responses to nearly every situation. Filled with doubt and despair, I questioned everything. Redemption seemed like a distant, impossible concept. I didn't think I could ever find a way to see myself as worthy or confident or to truly believe in my intrinsic goodness, and I didn't know if I could be the husband and father I aspired to be.

As I reflect on that dark moment, I realize that significant change — the deep, lasting transformation we all seek in our lives — doesn't happen quickly. It unfolds slowly, often painfully, over months and years rather than days or weeks. We all have dreams we want to chase, relationships we strive to nurture, and ideals we hope to embody. Yet, none of these aspirations materialize without sustained effort, perseverance, and patience.

Change, especially the kind that fundamentally alters who we are, requires time and relentless dedication. It's about more than just overcoming bad days or pushing through adversity; it's about a continuous commitment to growth and improvement. Whether it's repairing damaged relationships, building new skills, or reshaping our attitudes, the process is gradual. The spouse we want to be, the parent we aim to model — these roles demand our consistent attention and effort. The most valuable changes are those that are fought for, then painstakingly built with effort, and often, a fair share of failures. My journey has taught me that the path to redemption and personal fulfillment is long and fraught with challenges, but every step forward, no matter how small, is a victory.

A STRONG FOUNDATION TO WEATHER ANY STORM

After my "kitchen table moment," I understood I would need to fundamentally rebuild my entire house — physically and metaphorically — to achieve the peace and goals I sought. Establishing the right foundation for our lives means deconstructing our old ways and meticulously testing and experimenting with our beliefs. It involves deep introspection to discern our moral compass and identify the essential components that were absent the first time we laid our foundations.

In my life, this exploration required active engagement and determination. It was about pinpointing what was missing — whether it was faith, the ability to openly communicate my thoughts and feelings, or my reliance

Change, especially the

kind that fundamentally

alters who we are,

requires time and

relentless dedication.

on anger as a coping mechanism for life's challenges. These behaviors, while once seeming normal and even necessary, were, in fact, the very barriers preventing me from laying down a robust foundation that could support not just me but also my wife and our two children. Understanding and addressing these deficiencies were critical in building a new, lasting foundation that redefined how I interact with my world and the people in it. Each step, each discovery, brought me closer to creating a home — a life — that was not only structurally sound but also harmonious and fulfilling.

Recognizing the issues and identifying the missing elements in your foundation takes considerable time. For me, finding the right combination to establish a robust foundation for my home took years longer than I anticipated. However, I harbor no regrets about the time invested, as I am now confident that my foundation can withstand any of life's storms or challenges.

Once your foundation is solidly in place, the next step is rebuilding the house, which is a complex task because it isn't just about the physical structure; it's about incorporating the needs and wishes of those around you into the design. It's about ensuring that everyone's voice is heard and considered in how the home — your shared life — should function.

Often, in marriages, one spouse might move into the proverbial house of the other, but few couples engage in deep discussions about jointly tearing down and reconstructing this metaphorical house to suit both partners. Such conversations are crucial for understanding what each person needs in order to feel loved, heard, and supported. Essential elements like compassion, empathy, understanding, patience, effective communication, and gratitude for the richness that family brings are foundational to this process.

This dialogue about rebuilding together and what it means for each member of the family is an ongoing journey. If you have children, you know that just as you adapt to their current phase, they change again. This evolution starts from infancy and continues indefinitely. As parents and partners, we must be willing to embrace who they are becoming and encourage their paths without constraining them to our expectations. Discussing your metaphorical house involves understanding what those around you need from you and ensuring your home is a place where they can find what they seek — whether it's a conversation, love, or simply a safe space. This is not a one-time task but a continual process of adaptation and growth, ensuring our home remains a sanctuary for all its inhabitants.

EMBRACING THE PROCESS

Too often, especially within the veteran community, people seek swift solutions to deep-seated desires for change. Whether it's improving mental health, forging stronger bonds with our children, losing weight, excelling in physical fitness, enhancing job performance, or becoming better spouses, parents, or partners, the allure of a quick fix is ever-present. There are always offerings that promise shortcuts, claiming they can expedite our journey to these goals.

However, I urge you to remember that meaningful change cannot be rushed. If genuine shortcuts existed, they would be the norm instead of the exception. More importantly, even if such shortcuts could magically transport us to our desired outcomes, they would not equip us with the necessary experiences or growth needed to thrive once we arrive. The trials and challenges we encounter are not merely obstacles; they are opportunities for profound personal development.

This growth process allows us to truly embody the changes we seek, reinforcing our capabilities and resilience. It's in the journey, not the destination, where we find the strength and character to sustain the improvements we make. When we allow ourselves the time to evolve naturally, without rushing through the transformative steps to reach our goals, we invite God's light to shine through us, illuminating our path and guiding us to genuine, lasting change. This approach not only ensures we are prepared for the new challenges that accompany our achievements but also enriches our experience, making our accomplishments even more rewarding.

Embracing the journey rather than fixating on the destination has been pivotal in preserving my marriage and has enabled us to celebrate our eighteenth wedding anniversary this past March. It's important to acknowledge that our marriage isn't flawless or a model for others to emulate uncritically. Like any partnership, we experience our individual ups and downs, face our personal and professional challenges, and navigate the complexities life throws at us — both separately and together. Some of these challenges require mutual support and understanding as we tackle them side by side.

It's in the journey, not the destination, where we find the strength and character to sustain the improvements we make.

Recognizing that we are independent thinkers and won't always sync up perfectly is crucial for the health of our relationship. We don't always choose the best reaction. We are human — flawed and imperfect. Yet, it's this very acknowledgement and acceptance that strengthens our bond. We celebrate each other's dreams and aspirations with genuine enthusiasm and support, knowing how vital this is to both of us. Even when one of us might not handle a situation well, our shared foundation — built over time with patience and concerted effort — allows us to meet each other with grace, love, and humility. It's because of this solid base that we can support one another even when it's challenging and help each other progress toward who we need to be.

Our eighteenth anniversary symbolized not just a milestone of time spent together but of friendship, partnership, and mutual respect. Jenn is the first person I turn to with both good news and bad, and I am the same for her. The prospect of living without the other is something neither of us wants to face as we recognize the immense value our relationship brings to our lives. Thus, we persist in strengthening our bond, continually striving to improve our marriage and hold each other accountable to become the best versions of ourselves. This ongoing effort is not just about maintaining stability but about growing together, enriching our lives, and reinforcing the love that has sustained us through nearly two decades.

The day I exchanged vows with Jenn, I committed wholeheartedly, not just to the romance of the moment, but to the enduring journey of love, understanding, and mutual support. My vows were a solemn promise: "I, Eric, take you, Jennifer, to be my wife. To have and to hold from this day forward, for better, for worse, for richer, for poorer, in sickness and in health, to love and to cherish, until we are parted by death." Every word was laden with sincerity. However, I quickly learned that fulfilling these vows would demand more than just dedication; it required confronting personal demons and continuously striving to not only honor but also enrich our bond.

I believe society could do more to acknowledge the effort involved in maintaining a marriage. While it's not about placing married couples on a pedestal, there is immense value in recognizing the hard work, commitment, and resilience required to sustain such a relationship over decades. Celebrating this achievement should be about respecting the dedication it takes to build and maintain a healthy, enduring partnership that withstands the test of time and life's inevitable challenges.

Not only has working through my physical and mental struggles allowed me to enhance my relationship with my wife, but I've also grown into the father I always aspired to be. Finding the right balance of love, compassion, and discipline has been key to guiding my children as they navigate the complexities of the world. The truth is, despite the plethora of books claiming to have all the answers, parenting doesn't come with a manual. Many parenting trends today stem from such literature, yet often, when I read these theories, I find myself skeptical.

Over time, I've realized the most crucial approach to raising well-adjusted children is ensuring their needs for love, compassion, and appropriate discipline are met. This foundation fosters a profound and rewarding relationship founded on honesty — honesty in your words, your actions, your discipline, and your expectations. It's about aligning how you behave with what you expect from your children, ensuring your actions promote their best interests and setting the example.

While I celebrate the wonderful relationship I have with my children today, I'm aware that parenting is an ongoing process. Each day presents new opportunities for growth and learning for both me and my children. I continuously strive to improve, to humble myself, and to teach them valuable life skills and coping mechanisms. This ongoing effort ensures I can provide them with the stability and guidance they'll need throughout their lives. By committing to this path of continuous self-improvement and honest reflection, I not only uphold my role as their father but also prepare to support them as they grow and change.

Over the past eight years, my deepening faith has not only strengthened my bonds with my wife and children but has also transformed me into a better individual. This journey of spiritual growth reminds me vividly of the profound encounter I had with Jesus during my first No Barriers Warriors expedition. In that pivotal moment, as I surrendered my struggles and asked Him to lead my life, He revealed to me a vision of my garden, a sanctuary offering respite and peace, where I could truly feel God's love. It's easy to obstruct our own paths, as I often did before my transformative encounter with Jesus. And since then, I've prayed earnestly for guardrails from God to signal when I'm straying off the path He intended for me. I asked for a clear, unmistakable sign that would force me to reassess my actions or plans.

The response from God to such prayers isn't always immediate, which can fuel skepticism about His existence. However, the absence of an immediate reply doesn't imply He isn't listening or taking notes. Over the years, He has ingeniously provided the guardrails I prayed for. The recurring dream I described in the first chapter of this book serves as a potent reminder, a vivid warning signal. Whenever I find myself veering away from the path that aligns with His light, that dream invades my sleep. It appears when I neglect the small signs He sends throughout my day, when I fail to act justly toward others, or when I need to make amends for my shortcomings. After years of nurturing my faith and tending to my spiritual garden, I no longer question God's existence; I affirm it with conviction. Before my encounter with Jesus, I seldom spoke of my faith openly. Now, I declare my belief in God when asked and attest to the countless instances I've witnessed Him shouldering my burdens when they seemed unbearable.

My journey through faith has taught me that trusting in a higher power is crucial, especially when moving beyond traumatic experiences. An initial spark of faith in the goodness of humanity evolved into a profound, unshakable belief in the Creator, which allows me to face life's highs and lows with a mindset of gratitude, hope, and confidence that each challenge will lead to personal growth and strength.

I genuinely hope that on your journey, you discover this kind of faith — a faith that enables you to approach every situation with optimism and the assurance that something better awaits. By choosing love, compassion, empathy, and patience, you will emerge from any challenge stronger and more enriched. Conversely, if anger is your guide, you may find yourself lost in an endless maze, forever searching without finding your way out. True freedom and understanding come when you stop chasing fleeting desires and start navigating life's labyrinth with a clear, hopeful heart.

Never Quit! Always Move Forward!

ACKNOWLEDGEMENTS

I WANT TO extend my deepest gratitude to my mom, Lynne, and dad, Michael, for all the love and support they have given me. Your unwavering belief in me has transformed you into two of my closest friends. Your encouragement and belief in my dreams have been my foundation, making everything possible. Mom and Dad, your love has been my anchor, and I am forever grateful for your presence in my life.

Thank you to my mother-in-law, Karleen, and father-in-law, Rich, for your support and kindness. Your love and encouragement have meant a lot to me on this journey. ·

A sincere thank you to Erik Weihenmayer for writing the foreword on such a tight deadline. Your presence in my life and your constant availability for advice have been invaluable to my growth. I am deeply grateful for our friendship and for your unwavering support over the years.

To Curt, Martha, and the entire team at Life Elements, thank you for being a part of my world and for your generous sharing of time, knowledge, resources, and amazing products. Your support has profoundly impacted my life and helped me to gradually find my faith. Curt, I am especially grateful for the countless hours of business mentoring and marketing advice — I have learned so much from you. Finally, thank you for sponsoring my trip to Nepal in 2018. Without your generosity, there would have been no wheelchairs sent to Nepal.

A heartfelt thanks to James Geering for the unexpected phone call that reignited my motivation and set me on the path to make this climb. Your spontaneous encouragement came at just the right moment and made a significant impact on my journey.

To my dear friend Heather Thomson, thank you for teaching me so much about myself and what I am capable of as an entrepreneur. You saw potential in me long before I did and equipped me with the tools I needed to make this my reality. Thank you!

Maureen, thank you for being the life and business coach I needed. Your insights and friendship have always meant the world to me. I think of you every time I see the name of one of my companies.

Remembrance, I wouldn't be where I am without your guidance during those first few years of trying to find my way. You taught me so much about the hustle and grind and how to uplift those around me. I still use the skills you taught me every day in my business and life, and I am grateful our paths have crossed.

A heartfelt thank you to Rev. Rob Fuquay and my St. Luke's United Methodist Church family. Your unwavering support and prayers have been a source of immense strength and hope. Rev. Rob, your guidance and compassion have deeply impacted my journey. I am truly grateful for the love and encouragement from my church community. Thank you for being my rock and helping me find the light within.

To the individuals who have helped shape my life and influenced who I am today, I am profoundly thankful. Ed Weihenmayer, Jeremy Butler, Tom Porter, Wayne Hanson, Todd Andrews, No Barriers USA, Life Elements, *tasc* Performance, ROC Wheels, The Wheelchair Foundation, and many others — your guidance, support, and wisdom have empowered me with perspectives and tools I never had before. Your impact on my life is immeasurable, and I hold each of you in my heart with deep gratitude.

Thank you to my Great-Aunt Marcia for the many heartfelt conversations about faith at crucial moments around your kitchen table. Your wisdom and guidance have deeply nurtured my spiritual growth and strengthened my faith.

Thank you to Aunt Alice and Uncle Doug for always showing up for my family. Your love is treasured, as are you.

A special thank you to the entire medical team that has provided me with extraordinary care. Dr. Natalie Marshall; Dr. Laura Grabowski; Nicci Wilhoite, FNP; and Maria Renner, LMT, your dedication, compassion, and expertise have kept me upright and active, allowing me to live a full and vibrant life. You mean the world to me, and I wouldn't be where I am today without your exceptional care and support.

To the amazing team at Niche Pressworks, thank you for believing in this book with such enthusiasm and dedication. Your support has pushed me beyond my comfort zone and challenged me to explore new possibilities. Working with you has been an exhilarating journey, and I have cherished every moment of our collaboration.

Paulette, thank you for being a beautiful human, but especially for the advice. I will never forget it or you.

Brian, thank you for being one of the best neighbors I've ever had. Your generosity with your time is very much appreciated, but it's all the jokes we share that have made living next to you truly awesome.

To General Garrett, Colonel Keaveny, and Lieutenant Colonel Meier, thank you for taking the time from your insanely busy schedules to support me and *Canyon of Hope*. Words could never express the gratitude I have for you all or how much you each have taught me about being a good leader. General Garrett, thank you for the phone call and the solid advice it was timely and within a day found myself falling back on it.

To everyone who has touched my life and contributed to this journey, thank you. This book is a testament to the love, support, and inspiration I have received from so many wonderful people. Your influence has been a guiding force, and I am eternally grateful for every one of you.

ABOUT THE AUTHOR

ERIC DONOHO is a shining example of resilience and purpose-driven living. With a background that spans military service, sales and marketing, construction management, real estate, and dedicated volunteer work, Eric's story is one of overcoming challenges and helping others do the same.

As a retired Sergeant in the US Army, Eric earned several honors, including the Purple Heart, two Army Commendation Medals, two Army Achievement Medals, the Good Conduct Medal, the National Defense Service Medal, the Operation Iraqi Freedom Campaign Medal with Star, the Global War on Terror Service Medal, the Valorous Unit Award, and the Combat Infantry Badge. His military career was marked by bravery and an unbreakable spirit, even in the face of severe injuries.

After his military service, Eric founded Hand Up LLC and Hand Up Realty, where he combines his business success with a strong commitment to helping communities. His approach to business has always been to be honest and upfront and to provide real value to those needing his services, which is what has made him so successful.

CONTACT INFORMATION

WEBSITE: ericdonoho.com
EMAIL: info@handupllc.com
LINKEDIN: linkedin.com/in/ebdonoho
FACEBOOK: facebook.com/edonoho
INSTAGRAM: instagram.com/ebdonoho
X: x.com/ebdonoho

IF YOU ENJOYED this book, please consider leaving a review online at Amazon or wherever you purchased it. Without your support, this book will get lost among the thousands published each day. By leaving a positive review, you're not just helping me but also aiding fellow readers in discovering this book. Your feedback is invaluable and ensures that our shared message reaches more people. Together, we can make a difference. Thank you for being part of this journey and for going the extra mile with me!

FOR AMAZON (KINDLE) REVIEWS, SCAN HERE:

https://qr1.be/2R29

AFTER READING THIS BOOK, if you're inspired to work together —
whether for speaking engagements, joining my dynamic,
nationwide real estate team at *eXp Realty*, finding your
dream home or investment property, or seeking the perfect
real estate agent worldwide — let's connect!

Scan the QR Code below to connect with me or use the
contact information below. Be sure to mention that you're
reaching out because of *Canyon of Hope*. Together, we can
achieve incredible things!

https://qr1.be/19ZB

HAND UP LLC
4000 W 106th Street Suite 125-339
Carmel IN 46032
(317)379-9680
info@handupllc.com

EXPLORE THE BREATHTAKING photos from my journeys, including the cover photo of this book, *Canyon of Hope*. Scan the QR code to explore and purchase these mesmerizing prints, bringing the beauty of nature into your home. Don't miss the chance to own a piece of this visual journey!

https://qr1.be/ZI14

LET'S CONNECT ON social media! Scan the QR Code for all my links.

https://qr1.be/RF7P

Made in the USA
Middletown, DE
23 August 2024

59625370R00117